STRATEGIC STUDIES INSTITUTE

The Strategic Studies Institute (SSI) is part of the U.S. Army War College and is the strategic-level study agent for issues related to national security and military strategy with emphasis on geostrategic analysis.

The mission of SSI is to use independent analysis to conduct strategic studies that develop policy recommendations on:

- Strategy, planning, and policy for joint and combined employment of military forces;

- Regional strategic appraisals;

- The nature of land warfare;

- Matters affecting the Army's future;

- The concepts, philosophy, and theory of strategy; and,

- Other issues of importance to the leadership of the Army.

Studies produced by civilian and military analysts concern topics having strategic implications for the Army, the Department of Defense, and the larger national security community.

In addition to its studies, SSI publishes special reports on topics of special or immediate interest. These include edited proceedings of conferences and topically-oriented roundtables, expanded trip reports, and quick-reaction responses to senior Army leaders.

The Institute provides a valuable analytical capability within the Army to address strategic and other issues in support of Army participation in national security policy formulation.

i

Strategic Studies Institute
and
U.S. Army War College Press

DANGEROUS GROUND:
THE SPRATLY ISLANDS AND U.S. INTERESTS
AND APPROACHES

Clarence J. Bouchat

December 2013

*****

Comments pertaining to this report are invited and should be forwarded to: Director, Strategic Studies Institute and U.S. Army War College Press, U.S. Army War College, 47 Ashburn Drive, Carlisle, PA 17013-5010.

*****

This manuscript was funded by the U.S. Army War College External Research Associates Program. Information on this program is available on our website, *www.StrategicStudies Institute.army.mil*, at the Opportunities tab.

*****

All Strategic Studies Institute (SSI) and U.S. Army War College (USAWC) Press publications may be downloaded free of charge from the SSI website. Hard copies of this report may also be obtained free of charge while supplies last by placing an order on the SSI website. SSI publications may be quoted or reprinted in part or in full with permission and appropriate credit given to the U.S. Army Strategic Studies Institute and U.S. Army War College Press, U.S. Army War College, Carlisle, PA. Contact SSI by visiting our website at the following address: *www.StrategicStudiesInstitute.army.mil.*

*****

The Strategic Studies Institute and U.S. Army War College Press publishes a monthly email newsletter to update the national security community on the research of our analysts, recent and forthcoming publications, and upcoming conferences sponsored by the Institute. Each newsletter also provides a strategic commentary by one of our research analysts. If you are interested in receiving this newsletter, please subscribe on the SSI website at *www.StrategicStudiesInstitute.army.mil/newsletter.*

ISBN 1-58487-604-2

FOREWORD

Renewed interest in the Asia-Pacific region entails greater U.S. responsibilities and involvement in the area's problems. Of all the issues the United States will face in the region, none may involve as many players; legal, economic, and security interests; intricate considerations; historic implications; or persistent, if low key, conflict as the intractable disputes around the Spratly Islands. And none of the issues are probably as poorly understood by U.S. policymakers as the South China Sea disputes.

For these reasons, the Strategic Studies Institute (SSI) is pleased to publish this timely analysis of the Spratly Islands dispute. It examines the economic and security importance of the region to the surrounding claiming states: the People's Republic of China, Taiwan, Vietnam, Malaysia, Brunei, and the Philippines, and the violent acts and potential for instability in the region that has resulted. To better understand the positions of these parties, this monograph then delves into the customary international law claims for sovereignty through historic and occupation doctrines, and the subsequent maritime jurisdiction claims made through the United Nations Convention on the Law of the Sea. U.S. interests and resulting involvement are also explained to better understand these positions and inform U.S. policymakers on actions the United States may take to promote peace and economic development in an important region consisting of allies and crucial trading and security partners. This monograph then makes practical suggestions to directly improve U.S. security and economic interests in the region. SSI will publish a second monograph on the South China Sea disputes around the Paracel Islands to complement this analysis.

In the end, the conflict in the Spratly Islands is not one for the United States to solve, but its ability to contribute, facilitate, balance, or to support is necessary toward a solution from which all may benefit in the long term.

DOUGLAS C. LOVELACE, JR.
Director
Strategic Studies Institute and
   U.S. Army War College Press

ABOUT THE AUTHOR

CLARENCE J. BOUCHAT is a retired U.S. Air Force officer and currently a senior researcher with the Strategic Studies Institute and an adjunct professor at the U.S. Army War College (USAWC) Department of Distance Education. His last assignment was as a faculty member of the USAWC. He served in several assignments in East Asia and has published articles about the region. Lieutenant Colonel (Retired) Bouchat is a graduate of the U.S. Air Force Academy and the University of Southern California.

SUMMARY

The region around the Spratly Islands and the South China Sea is important to the economies of the surrounding states in terms of fish resources and the potential for natural gas and oil. This bonanza of riches spurs out-sized claims in the region that result in diplomatic and physical clashes. The large flow of maritime commerce around the Spratly Islands is also crucial to the economic well-being of the region and the world, and occupation of the islands dictates control of the surrounding sea's maritime traffic, security, and economic exploitation. Their importance is seen in the 50 remote military garrisons on these islets by the claiming states, and the decades-long history of military and civilian enforcement clashes which increase the risk of conflict.

The use of customary law and the United National Convention on the Law of the Sea (UNCLOS) in establishing claims to the Spratlys and surrounding waters helps explain the perspectives of the disputants. Their legal positions are especially important for American policymakers as they inform possible solutions and suggest how to contribute to peace and prosperity in the region. Three key legal questions must be answered to help sort the disputes: sovereignty over the islets, the nature of a claimed land feature, and the delimitation of maritime jurisdiction. Sovereignty is claimed through customary law, with the People's Republic of China (PRC), Taiwan, and Vietnam using historic doctrine to claim the entire South China Sea, while they also use the doctrine of occupation to claim some land features, the method which the Philippines and Malaysia also employ. Each are also disputed with counterclaims by other South China Sea states, leaving no state holding effective legal sovereignty over all.

Once sovereignty and feature type are determined, zones of authority may be established by the occupying state, depending on the distance from its established shore baseline. Internal, archipelagic, and historic waters are maritime variations of near-full sovereign control, which could be disruptive to economic and navigation activities if awarded to Vietnam or China, both of which make such claims. Islands above the high tide mark establish territorial waters and a contiguous zone, which would carve 24 nautical mile (nm) zones like Swiss cheese around the Spratlys, but should allow innocent passage. The length of the 200-nm exclusive economic zone (EEZ) allows much potential overlap among land masses and islands in the semi-enclosed South China Sea, and, like territorial waters, some states restrict military activities within the EEZ. Although such arguments by claimants for more restrictions in these zones are tenuous, they could be useful justification to cover military actions by states like the PRC, which is the most active in enforcing a restrictive EEZ.

Freedom of navigation in the South China Sea is the most immediate concern for the United States to ensure naval vessels retain all rights of access. Current policy in China, Vietnam, and Malaysia restrict foreign naval activities in their zones beyond those normally attributed to UNCLOS. Concluding an *Incidents at Sea Agreement* with the PRC would clarify the rights and responsibilities between the two. Other forms of government to government interaction could build confidence in present and future agreements, and leverage common interests. U.S. ratification of UNCLOS is another important step to influence the evolution of future interpretations of freedom of navigation toward more open use. Although a more difficult proposition, the United States should demand the clarification of the historic claims made in the South China Sea so as to facilitate negotiating a settlement, and accelerate economic development.

Open economic access to the South China Sea maritime commons is a second U.S. interest, but one which may diverge from freedom of navigation. Access to the resources of the high seas is an important enough U.S. interest to stall U.S. ratification of UNCLOS for nearly 20 years. While the United States remains outside the treaty, however, it holds less influence over how maritime law is interpreted and evolves, and thus is at a disadvantage to shape events like whether the South China Sea becomes a wholly divided and claimed sea. Such arrangements as a Joint Development Zone or a Joint Management Zone could stabilize the area and facilitate economic development for its participants. To support any of the joint development solutions, the United States would have to place its security interests over potential economic ones.

To contribute to overall stability and prosperity in the region, the United States must delicately play the roles of conciliator and balancer as circumstances require. The United States is an honest broker because it shares goals in common with the states around the South China Sea. Although the United States may not be truly neutral, it has less direct demands in the disputes, garnered more trust than most other states, and possesses resources to bear on these issues, making it a useful interlocutor in resolving problems.

In other circumstances, the United States has intervened in problems around the Spratly Islands in more parochial ways to balance the diplomatic field in aid of allies and defense partners and to directly protect its freedom of navigation interests. This balancer role should deter aggression, is dictated by U.S. treaty obligation to the Philippines, and is needed because the Association of Southeast Asian Nations (ASEAN) lacks a defense arrangement by which to counter the influence of the PRC. The balancing role, however, should be minimal so as to not to overshadow the conciliator role.

The United States has again made the Asia-Pacific region a major focus of its stated global interests, and converging national interests between the United States and China may indicate that some progress on the issues outlined here are possible. The importance of the Spratly Islands region to world trade, energy, and security, as well as its own national interests require careful American involvement. To best address the disputes, policymakers must understand the underlying territorial and maritime claims of the PRC, Taiwan, Vietnam, Malaysia, Indonesia, Brunei, and the Philippines in order to help manage these issues peacefully and equitably for the regional states, and to meet U.S. interests. In the end, the conflict in the Spratly Islands is not one for the United States to solve, but its ability to contribute, facilitate, balance, or support is necessary toward a solution from which all may benefit.

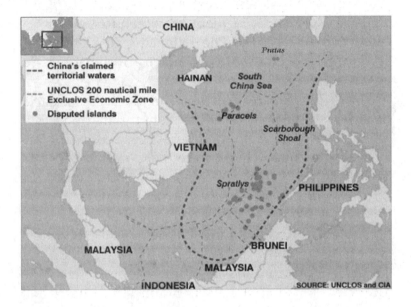

Source: David Lai, *The United States and China in Power Transition*, Carlisle, PA: Strategic Studies Institute, U.S. Army War College, December 2011.

Map 1. South China Sea.

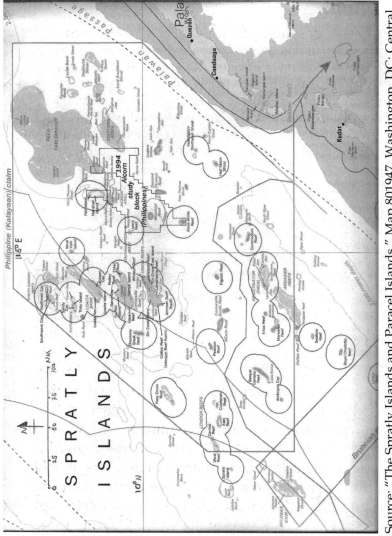

Source: "The Spratly Islands and Paracel Islands," Map 801947, Washington, DC: Central
Intelligence Agency (CIA), December 1995.

Map 2. The Spratley Islands.

DANGEROUS GROUND:
THE SPRATLY ISLANDS AND U.S. INTERESTS
AND APPROACHES

> Whoever dominates the sea dominates world trade;
> whoever dominates world trade dominates the Gol-
> conda [a location of great wealth]; whoever dominates
> the Golconda dominates the world. . . . Boost the ship-
> ping industry to expand the navy, let our national
> navy keep pace with the big powers and get into the
> rank of first-class powers. The only way for China to
> become prosperous is to develop its military arms.[1]

> Sun Yat-sen,
> Founder and first President
> of the Republic of China

The South China Sea is one of the most strategic waterways in the world, for its sea lanes have been heavily used by fisherman, merchantmen, and war ships for 2,000 years. During that time, its tiny groupings of islets, reefs, banks, cays, shoals, atolls, and exposed rocks constituting the Maccelesfield Bank, Scarborough Shoal, and Paratas, Paracel, and Spratly Islands have posed deadly hazards to navigation that tarred this region with the maritime epithet of "the Dangerous Ground."[2] Although modern navigation has reduced the risk of shipwreck in the region, it remains a junction where international interests and rivalries clash—sometimes quite violently—keeping the name of "Dangerous Ground" a politically apt one. The waters and islets of the South China Sea suffer conflicting claims in whole or in part made by the People's Republic of China (PRC), Republic of China (ROC or Taiwan), Vietnam, the Philippines, Malaysia, Indonesia, and Brunei, and are vital international

1

waters for maritime states like India, Australia, the Republic of Korea (South Korea), Japan, and the United States. The bitter nature of the claims to this area, which possesses rich fish stocks, oil and natural gas potential, and security importance, markedly increases their significance to the claimants in southeastern Asia, and to other nautical powers with interests in the high seas and stability in this rapidly developing strategic region.

Because the Spratly Islands are an especially complicated, emotional, and central part of the South China Sea disputes, this monograph delves into why this tiny archipelago warrants better understanding by U.S. policymakers in order to discuss nuanced responses to the region's challenges. To attain that needed understanding, legal aspects of customary and modern laws are explored to analyze the differences between competing maritime and territorial claims, and why and how the parties involved stake rival claims or maritime legal rights. Throughout, the policies of the United States are examined through its conflicted interests in the region. Recommendations for how the United States should engage these issues, a more appropriate task than trying to solve the disputes outright, are then offered. Since the problems in the waters around the Spratly Islands are daunting enough, dealing with the other disputed parts of the South China Sea are left for further study, although many topics discussed here may also be gainfully applied elsewhere in the region. U.S. contributions to regional solutions are predicated upon a better understanding of the many issues involved.

THE SPRATLY ISLANDS REGION AND WHY IT IS IMPORTANT

The South China Sea is a body of water in Southeast Asia partially enclosed by the continental coasts of Vietnam and China, and portions of the shores of Taiwan, the Philippines, Malaysia, Brunei, and Indonesia. Hundreds of tiny geologic features dot the 122,648,000 square nautical miles (nm^2) of the South China Sea, or one and half times the size of the Mediterranean Sea, although its largest natural grouping, the approximately 170[3] features of the Spratly Islands archipelago, covers a total of less than 3 nm^2 of land above sea level nestled in an area spanning 58,000 nm^2 of sea.[4] The Spratly Islands are centered in the southern half of the South China Sea approximately 300-nm east of Vietnam, 200-nm west of the Philippines, and 800-nm south of the Chinese mainland. The core Spratlys grouping stretches 315-nm from northern Northeast Cay to southern Louisa Reef, and 240-nm from western Ladd Reef to eastern Investigator Northeast Shoal. The ocean floor in this area is relatively shallow compared to the much deeper northern half, but is mostly cut off from the surrounding continental shelves by troughs as deep as 5,000 meters.[5] Although unremarkable in its composition, the physical proximity and characteristics of these features, surrounding waters, and ocean floor play a very important role in the disputes of the region and potential ways to address them.

Local Economic Importance of the Spratly Region.

Joining the Pacific and Indian Oceans, the warm South China Sea is among the most biologically diverse areas in the world, rich in both endangered species and commercial fish like tuna, mackerel, scads, and coral reef fish.[6] The South China Sea is one of the earth's most productive fishing zones in terms of its annual maritime catch representing about 10 percent of the world's total take, and contributes about half of the fish eaten in the Philippines, Vietnam, and China—especially in poorer coastal areas.[7] Seafood was also Vietnam's second largest foreign exchange earner in 2010 accounting for 7 percent of its exports, and composed over 4 percent of the Philippines' gross domestic product (GDP) in 2009.[8] The nature of the partially enclosed South China Sea and migratory nature of these fish stocks mean this important source of food and trade is a shared resource among the bordering states posing a "tragedy of the commons" dilemma in managing its stocks and genetic sustainability.[9] Since the late-1990s, over-fishing, coral reef damage, and coastal and shipping pollution have threatened the sustainability of fishing in the South China Sea, with no substantial international coordination yet in place to halt continuing dwindling of fishing stocks.[10] Instead, declining stocks in home waters have forced fisherman into waters claimed by other states, precipitating adverse reactions by maritime law enforcement officials in order to protect the commercial interests within their claimed areas. Fishing-related incidents thus are common in the South China Sea and sometimes lead to diplomatic or armed clashes.[11]

The extraction of hydrocarbon energy resources in the South China Sea also suffers under the tension of being an asset of the maritime commons. The shallower southern South China Sea, which includes the Spratly Islands, has been called a "second Persian Gulf" or "hydrocarbons Eldorado" for its rich potential.[12] Certainly the possibility for energy strikes in the area's sedimentary basins exists. However, the Spratly Islands region itself remains largely unexplored so estimates vary widely.[13] The U.S. Energy Information Administration (USEIA) in 2013 gives proven or probable reserves in the Spratly region at virtually none for oil and only .1 trillion cubic feet (tcf) for natural gas. However, USEIA estimated the potential for undiscovered oil at between .8 and 5.4 billion barrels (bbl) and 7 to 55 tcf for gas. The PRC's Chinese National Offshore Oil Company (CNOOC) offers a far more optimistic estimate of 125 bbl of oil and 500 tcf of gas in undiscovered resources,[14] which is five times China's current proven reserves in both resources. This may be skewed in order to encourage investment and exploration since China's domestic production has peaked, and it depends heavily on imported energy.[15] China needs the "sweeter" crude oil that comes from the South China Sea because it is easier for overburdened Chinese refineries to process, makes China more energy independent as its demand for oil doubles and natural gas quadruples in the next 25 years, and reduces the debilitating air pollution of burning coal which now accounts for much of its energy.[16]

The exploration for oil in the vicinity of the Spratly Islands started in the 1970s around Reed Bank by a Philippine consortium including U.S. companies, but the results were meager. The PRC started drilling in 1992 near Vanguard Bank, using the American company, Crestone, while just to the west, the Vietnamese explored the Blue Dragon block with Mobil, and to the southeast, Malaysia contracted with Sabah Shell.[17] Further afield in the South China Sea, commercial drilling proceeds in Malaysia's Central Luconia gas fields off the coast of Sarawak, in Indonesia's Natuan Island gas field, and Vietnam's Lan Tay and Lan

Do (or Nam Con Son) gas fields.[18] The Philippine's Malampaya field, northwest of Palawan island and just outside the Spratlys area, may hold 2.7 tcf of natural gas reserves, but is the only producing gas field in the Spratly region.[19] The belief that such finds may extend to the Spratly Islands' waters, whose central placement makes maritime possession uncertain, encourages the affected parties to make competing, sometimes outsized, claims for this wealth.[20]

The richest part of the Spratlys may be shallow Reed Bank, in the northeast corner and only 150-nm from the Philippine's Palawan Island, but it is also claimed by the PRC, Taiwan, and Vietnam. After natural gas was discovered there in 2002, the Philippines assigned concessions for its development; however, Chinese pressure has halted subsequent activities in Reed Bank.[21] Such overlapping claims make financing and exploration to confirm potential energy reserves in the region more costly and risky, as demonstrated by Beijing's threats to the businesses of foreign companies in China if they help develop the stakes of other claimants.[22] Further complicating the problem is that more than 200 international companies are contracted for oil and natural gas services in the greater South China Sea region which internationalizes and complicates the dispute because China disapproves of foreign companies being involved in the region.[23] International energy companies have the expertise needed to develop these waters but remain reluctant to do so, needing long-term stability in the region.[24] The potential for major energy finds in the Spratly Islands area has driven the energy-poor but rapidly developing surrounding states to press aggressive claims for this disputed commons which, in turn, hobbles their efforts by making exploration and exploitation economically more risky, politically contentious, and militarily dangerous.[25]

Unfortunately, the states claiming this area "view the competition for access to and ownership of the resources as a zero-sum game."[26] For instance, after the 2008 dissolution of the disappointing Joint Maritime Seismic Undertaking (JMSU), the first and only multilateral cooperative development arrangement among the South China Sea states, its former members, Vietnam, the Philippines, and the PRC, began to explore unilaterally in their overlapping claimed areas, and China increased the number of its enforcement vessels in the region.[27] Claims have intensified as new technology has made previously difficult offshore oil and gas more accessible, while high energy prices make their potential more lucrative.[28] Thus political and armed clashes may occur in order to develop this energy potential before others exploit it first.

If the waters around the Spratlys have historically been rich fishing grounds and today portend hydrocarbon wealth, the land features themselves have offered much less in economic activities and have never been permanently inhabited beyond recent military garrisons.[29] The earliest visitors to the Spratlys may have been Chinese traders collecting feathers and tortoise shells, but most of the early Chinese references to the South China Sea mainly warned of the danger from the reefs, and the geologic features served mostly as landmarks to navigators and occasional shelter to fisherman.[30] In 1877, Britain made probably the first Western-style claim to any of the islands for the southerly Spratly Island and Amboyna Cay to exploit their guano deposits (for use in making fertilizer and soap).[31] Tomas Cloma started the Philippines' unofficial claim to most of the Spratlys in 1947 also in order to gather guano and to establish a fish cannery.[32] None of these activities were seriously pursued. The climate and tiny land area available in the Spratlys offers little agricultural promise, although the Taiwanese have grown pineapples on Itu Aba, the largest island in the Spratly group, and Vietnam has experimented with growing trees for shade and fencing on its occupied islets.[33] Some experts see the possibility for marine based tourism in the region, such as Malaysia has done for its human-enhanced Swallow Reef which has become a premier dive resort sharing space with a military installation and airstrip.[34] Collectively, transnational ecotourism has been targeted through the Brunei-Indonesia-Malaysia-Philippines East Association of Southeast Asian Nations (ASEAN) Growth Area (BIMP-EAGA) through government and private sector investment that could be followed in the South China Sea.[35] However, all of this collecting, farming, and tourism potential of the land features financially pales in comparison to the surrounding waters' fishing and drilling activities. The islets have yet to produce any sustained economic yield, or as Timo Kivimaki concludes in his anthology on the South China Sea, "these areas have only been economically meaningful when the small reefs and islands have disrupted sea lines of communication."[36]

Regional Security Importance of the Spratlys.

Although economically not significant, the land features of the Spratlys may hold military importance for the states occupying or claiming them. The historically high amount of shipping which transits the South China Sea gives significance to the Spratly Islands for sea lane defense, maritime interdiction, early warning, and surveillance. During World War II, Japanese imperial forces claimed all and occupied key parts of the South China Sea, constructing a submarine support base on Itu Aba as part of their efforts to successfully cut Allied shipping in the region. The islets also served as forward staging bases for invasions of the Philippines, the Dutch East Indies (now Indonesia), and Malaya.[37] From 1840 to 1949, one Chinese scholar counted 479 attacks launched against China from the sea, with 84 of those being major assaults.[38] During the Vietnam War, U.S. bomber and surveillance missions were flown from Guam and Okinawa over the South China Sea, which China and North Vietnam protested as violating each one's sovereignty.[39] This military legacy particularly menaces modern China's prosperity since 50 percent of its petroleum is imported from overseas, and 90 percent of its foreign trade is through shipping, much through the South China Sea from China's booming southern provinces.[40] To counter this potential threat, Chinese military leaders consider the South China Sea important to the PRC's security, and their maritime "near sea strategy" is to neutralize any threat within the "first island chain," defined as a line connecting Borneo with the Philippine, Taiwan, Ryukyu, Japanese, and Kurile Islands, to ensure access to the Pacific Ocean and prevent a "Great Wall in reverse."[41] Having actually sustained attacks from the Spratly Islands, other South China Sea states also want to control some or all of the Spratly features for their own protection. For instance, since the 1980s, the Philippines government considers the adjacent Spratly group "vital to the defense of its western perimeter" and to its economic survival.[42] Such sentiment explains, in part, the regional land grab for otherwise uninhabited and unproductive land features. Territorial disputes have often been a motive for fighting between states, which is why one analyst dubbed the Spratly Islands "the least unlikely trigger" to start a conflict in the South China Sea.[43]

In order to defend national security and further their claims, Taiwan, Vietnam, the Philippines, Malaysia, and the PRC have garrisoned many of the Spratly features. Accurate numbers and dispositions for military forces are difficult to ascertain, but reasonably reliable numbers are reported here to portray their scope. A total of over 1,500 troops are probably deployed to between 45 and 52 positions in the Spratlys.[44] Following the abandonment of the Spratlys by the Japanese after World War II, the ROC was the first to occupy a position in 1946, but these forces were withdrawn after the Nationalist forces retreated to Taiwan.[45] In 1956, about 500 marines were re-stationed on Itu Aba, Taiwan's only occupation, but that force was reduced to 110 in the late-1990s. The islet was further demilitarized in 2000 by stationing only coast guardsmen there, although a 1,000 meter airstrip was completed in 2008 to allow rapid reinforcement.[46] In 1975, Vietnam occupied 13 positions, and today garrisons the most features at around 29, with about 600 troops. Vietnamese forces maintain a 600-meter runway on Spratly Island itself, the region's fourth largest island.[47] Since 1971, the Philippines has occupied eight to nine of its approximate 53 claimed geographical structures with about 500 marines (down from 1,000 in the 1990s), and completed a 1,300-meter runway in 1981 on Thitu Island, the region's second largest island.[48] Since 1983, Malaysia has manned five of its 12 claimed features with 70 soldiers. Its largest, the geographically enhanced Swallow Reef, also includes a 600-meter commercial and military airport.[49]

The PRC was late in joining the scramble in 1988, but has aggressively settled about seven reefs and rocks, some since upgraded with helipads.[50] Some of these features are close to those already occupied by other forces in a possible attempt to neutralize any claim by other states to the surrounding seas. The 1992 People's Liberation Army (PLA) landing on Da Ba Dau Reef, near Vietnamese occupied Sin Cowe East Island, resulted in a skirmish with nearby Vietnamese forces.[51] The PLA's 1995 seizure of Mischief Reef, previously abandoned by Philippine forces although within the Philippine's Alcorn oil concession area, significantly raised tensions between the two countries. Tensions flared again after construction of upgraded military structures on these rocks in 1998—although no actual fighting ensued either time.[52] A U.S. Government report placed the total contingent of Chinese marines at 325 in 1999, although other estimates report it as low as 260 personnel.[53] Many of the smaller outposts, especially the Chinese ones, are precarious manmade platforms perched above tiny rocks or even submerged reefs.[54] The seizure of features has stopped since the late-1990s, however, in part because the most suitable features are already occupied and because these remote desolate outposts are expensive to maintain.[55] A "no new garrisons" policy was reinforced by the nonbinding Declaration of the Conduct of Parties in the South China Sea (DOC) in which China and all 10 ASEAN states agree to nonuse of force, peaceful settlements, and to refrain from further manning unoccupied features.[56] In the spirit of the DOC, and despite the shortage of available real estate in the Spratly Islands, no country has attempted to drive off the troops of another country's occupied base.[57]

This relative acquiescence toward intermingled military-occupied features has not extended to defending maritime and economic interests in the surrounding seas, however. The Dangerous Ground has lived up to its name with numerous clashes and challenges over the past several decades. The PRC, with its extensive claims and most capable naval and maritime civilian forces, has been the most involved against other states' vessels, beginning with far-ranging naval patrols in 1987 throughout most of the South China Sea, protecting an area that China considers its "inherent territories."[58] The most deadly Spratlys clash occurred in 1988 when warships from the PLA Navy (PLAN) and Vietnam People's Navy (VPN) exchanged fire off Johnson Reef South with each side sinking a vessel and around 70 Vietnamese sailors lost.[59] This fight began a turbulent period in the South China Sea in which military forces played a prominent (although less lethal) role. For instance, in April 1994, a Vietnamese gunboat removed a Chinese research vessel from an area claimed by both countries, and in July, the PLAN blocked a Vietnamese-licensed oil rig.[60] From 1992 to 1996, Taiwan reported 134 incidents of its fishing fleet being boarded, harassed, detained, rammed, or fired upon by PLAN vessels in the northern South China Sea.[61] Tensions started to calm in 1995, however, when the PRC's foreign minister attended the ASEAN Regional Forum (ARF). Naval ships from all of the states have subsequently played a more subdued role in these waters.[62]

Instead of its navy, China has since used its maritime law enforcement ships to protect its claims, although backed by the PLAN which often shadows just over the horizon.[63] Five disparate PRC maritime enforcement agencies[64] have aggressively policed China's interests, and kept tensions high throughout the South China Sea. In 2013, the Chinese government consolidated four of these agencies into a single paramilitary coast guard under a new National Oceanic Administration, creating an "'iron fist' that would replace ineffective operations scattered among a number of agencies."[65] This streamlining may only partially rein in the aggressive nature of Chinese patrolling, since other ministries within China have conflicting views on the South China Sea disputes with the "policy of reactive assertiveness, characterized by strong reactions to provocations by other parties" still being practiced after the reorganization.[66] Whereas, before the consolidation only the Maritime Police agency was armed, in the new expanded coast guard, all of its vessels will be armed, increasing significantly the weaponry available.[67] In 2009, the PRC's South Sea Region Fisheries Administration Bureau detained 33 Vietnamese ships, and seven in 2010.[68] In one of five such incidents near Reed Bank in early 2011, two China Marine Surveillance ships aggressively maneuvered against a Philippine seismic survey ship, forcing it to leave the area. In May 2011, the Vietnamese claimed that a China Marine Surveillance ship cut the cables of a PetroVietnam oil and gas survey ship in disputed waters near Vietnam, and in June a Chinese fishing vessel intentionally rammed the exploration cables of another Vietnamese survey ship.[69] Just north of the Spratly Islands around Scarborough Shoal, a protracted 2-month standoff between PRC and Philippine vessels started in April 2012 over rights to enforce fishery resource rules that blocked vessels and increased already taut tensions.[70] Although events involving naval vessels have subsided, the level of police and commercial vessel incidents has increased as a result of China tripling its patrols at sea since 2008.[71] Some incidents have been attributed to Chinese fishing vessels, which can be an auxiliary to enforcement agencies as demonstrated in the 2012 Scarborough Shoal incident.[72] These pose different but serious problems because civilian vessels have been "easier to deploy, operate under looser chains of command, and engage more readily in skirmishes."[73] The U.S. Pacific Fleet Deputy Chief of Staff for Intelligence and Information, speaking at a conference in a personal capacity, recently warned that the PLAN is using its civilian proxies for "Maritime confrontations [that] haven't been happening close to the Chinese mainland. Rather, China is negotiating for control of other nations' resources off their coasts."[74] "It is a brilliant strategy by China to establish their control over an area without firing a single shot," observed Stephanie Kleine-Ahlbrandt, head of the Beijing office of the International Crisis Group.[75] PRC vessels have been active in enforcing China's maritime claims in the South China Sea, exacerbating the tensions among the states involved.

As the Scarborough Shoal standoff shows, numerous incidents are also initiated by the ASEAN claimants. For example, during the especially contentious period of the 1990s, the Philippine Navy sank a Chinese fishing boat in 1993; a Malaysian patrol boat fired on a Chinese trawler in 1995, injuring four men; and in 1999, Philippine naval vessels twice bumped Chinese fishing boats, all taking place in disputed areas.[76] Military incidents among the ASEAN states are rare, but one occurred in 1976 when Vietnamese forces on its then main garrison on Southwest Cay fired on a Philippines aircraft that flew too close, although without effect.[77] Another confrontation almost occurred in 1999 when aircraft from the Philippines and Malaysia "nearly engaged" over Malaysian controlled Investi-gator Shoal—although both afterwards dismissed the incident in more ASEAN-like conciliatory fashion.[78] Under civilian authorities, incidents occur with "In-creasingly assertive positions among claimants [that] have pushed regional tensions to new heights."[79] Ex-amples in this monograph have offered only a few of many altercations in contested waters consisting of Malaysian intervention against Philippine and Vietnamese fishing boats, Philippine actions against Vietnamese and Malaysian vessels, and Vietnam-ese enforcement of its claims against the others.[80] All have also forcibly reacted against Chinese commercial vessels as well.[81] Since 1989, more than 300 incidents against Chinese trawlers have been reported, includ-ing being fired upon, seized, or expelled, with 10 ships detained by the Vietnamese in 2010, for example.[82] De-spite the many disputes among ASEAN states in the South China Sea, however, there have been very few casualties among them—in contrast to clashes with the PRC.[83] As a relative lull in naval and police actions in the South China Sea during the 2000s seems to be ending, some analysts fear that a major discovery of energy resources could fan the flames of more serious clashes in a region lacking the mechanisms for con-flict management.[84] The International Crisis Group observes, "While the likelihood of major conflict re-mains low, all of the trends are in the wrong direc-tion, and prospects of resolution are diminishing."[85] Those assessments bode poorly for the region's states and for the United States, which also has significant interests there.

Importance of the Spratly Region to the United States.

In addition to the South China Sea region holding huge potential for producing oil and natural gas, it is also one of the world's great thoroughfares of energy and trade, and thus of immense importance to the United States and the international community. The United Nations (UN) Conference on Trade and Development estimated that 8.4 million tons of maritime trade, more than half of the world's annual total, passed into the South China Sea in 2010. The USEIA estimates that around 6 tcf of natural gas, over half of the world's maritime gas movement, was part of that trade, as was approximately 14 trillion barrels of oil, or a third of the world's volume.[86] These massive movements link energy rich southwest Asia and northern Africa to economically vibrant northeast Asia. An estimated 80 percent of Taiwanese, 66 percent of South Korean, and 60 percent of Japanese energy supplies are imported via the South China Sea, which also accounts for 40 percent of Japan's total exports and imports.[87] These busiest shipping lanes in the world pass by either side of the centrally placed Spratly Islands,[88] and their security is crucial to nearby states with which the United States has a range of formal defense arrangements including Taiwan, South Korea, Japan, Australia, the Philippines, Thailand, and Singapore.[89] Economic development in East Asia and the world would be seriously set back should maritime trade in the South China Sea be disrupted.[90] The PRC, ROC, and Vietnam each claim all of the Spratly Islands and most of the South China Sea, and these conflicting and extensive maritime claims also challenge U.S. economic interests to exploit water column and seabed resources on what many parties consider high seas or international waters.[91] U.S. economic interests are directly and indirectly entwined in the competition over the distant Spratly Islands.

As this monograph has shown, this region is not just another global hot spot, but one with important long-term economic, territorial, and security contentions. That makes it not just one of the world's most disputed ocean areas, but also one of the few where violent incidents routinely occur at sea.[92] For diplomatic, historic, and military capacity reasons, other states rely on the United States to ensure stability in the South China Sea.[93] This dependence could make the Spratlys a convenient arena in which a rising China may test U.S. political will and dominance through increasingly assertive incidents to which the United States must respond to protect partner and American security and economic interests.[94] A senior fellow at the Atlantic Council observed that:

> Some in China may have believed that the global financial crisis that started in late 2007 signaled the decline of the U.S. and that the time was ripe to become more assertive.[95]

Thus the United States may face the difficult dilemma of balancing its interests in support of allies and partners with protecting its political and economic relations with the PRC.[96] For these reasons, American journalist and Stratfor analyst Robert Kaplan dubbed the South China Sea the world's "new central theater of conflict," and "the heart of political geography in coming decades."[97] Yet mutual economic and political dependence among all of these states, and with the United States, argues against major conflict or even a Cold War-style rivalry.[98] Each state with interests in the South China Sea also understands the cooperative need for stability, sustainable management of resources, freedom of navigation, crime prevention, and a host of other common interests in the region which cannot be attained by force alone.[99] Indeed, the United States and PRC signed an agreement in 1998 entitled "Establishing a Consultation Mechanism to Strengthen Military Maritime Safety" (or the Military Maritime Consultative Agreement [MMCA]) to prevent incidents between them.[100] Nonetheless, concerns remain that strong motivations, existing tensions, and entrenched positions need only an accident or miscommunication to create an incident or open conflict that subjugates all of these interests.[101] Another reason why the South China Sea is important to the United States is that such incidents already occur.

Although ostensibly neutral and not a part of any of the land or maritime claims in the South China Sea, the United States and other seafaring states do have international rights in the area which have been challenged in contentious ways — the legal bases for which are explained in the next section. The comprehensive claims by the PRC to all of the waters of the South China Sea, and its government's interpretation of international law, encourages the Chinese to bar any activity by foreign military vessels and aircraft from what most other states determine to be high seas and transitable Chinese maritime jurisdictions.[102] Some analysts believe that U.S. surveillance actions in the northern South China Sea, which China contends trespass on its jurisdiction, risks drawing the United States into a conflict in the region.[103] Although this concern is now based on events in proximity to Chinese mainland waters, should the PRC prevail in its claims to land features and waters around the Spratly Islands, the entire South China Sea could become a Chinese lake off-limits to foreign government vessels without permission. Despite the deconfliction efforts of the 1998 MMCA, aggressive incidents have occurred between Chinese vessels and U.S. craft exercising freedom of navigation rights. The most serious incident was the 2001 collision of a Chinese fighter jet with a U.S. Navy EP-3 which killed the Chinese pilot, and forced the American crew to an emergency landing at the Chinese base on Hainan Dao.[104] On the surface, harassment by Chinese vessels has occurred against the U.S. ocean surveillance fleet, including the U.S. Naval Ships (USNS) *Bowditch* (2001 and 2002), *Bruce C. Heezen* (2003), *Victorious* (2003 and 2004), *Effective* (2004), *John McDonnell* (2005), *Mary Sears* (2005), *Loyal* (2005), and *Impeccable* (2009).[105] During this last incident, five Chinese vessels surrounded the hydrographic survey ship roughly 75 miles southeast of Hainan Dao, and attempted to snag its towing cable, to which the U.S. Navy responded by dispatching warships to escort subsequent unarmed survey and ocean surveillance vessels.[106] While this monograph went to print in December 2013, a renewed round of tensions seem to have started with the PRC establishing an air defense identification zone (ADIZ) over disputed islands in the East China Sea with the establishment of a similar ADIZ expected in the South China Sea, and a near-collision incident between the USS *Cowpens* and escort vessels of the PRC's Liaoning carrier battle group in disputed international waters of the South China Sea.[107] Even if the United States held absolute neutrality among the disputants, it might still be drawn into the South China Sea fracas to reinforce its maritime rights guaranteed under international law.

LEGAL BASIS AND CLAIMS IN THE SPRATLY ISLANDS SCRUM

What is the cause for this melee over land sovereignty, maritime jurisdiction, assertion of international rights, and police and military incidents around the Spratly Islands? To best understand the issues and in order to better contribute to their solution, this section analyzes customary (or traditional) law which governs disputes over sovereignty of land and some forms of maritime jurisdiction and rights, and the 1982 UN Convention on the Law of the Sea (UNCLOS) which only addresses maritime issues, but in a more comprehensive and coherent manner.[108] This section also examines how each of the involved parties applies these concepts to support its contentious claims. In this section, disputes over land sovereignty are generally treated distinctly from maritime jurisdiction disputes, although either claim may depend upon the legal standing of the other and may blur together in the case of historic claims, as will be shown.[109] Sovereignty determination over geologic features, boundary delimitation of maritime borders, and the nature of those features as productive islands or uninhabitable rocks are three crucial decisions over which the claimants contest.[110] Concepts here are covered to the depth needed to apply to the Spratly Islands and are not meant to be comprehensive. Complicating such an examination are the facts that international law is neither complete nor rigorous enough to be "a constitution" to consider the full merit of competing claims,[111] and some modern legal regimes may conflict with customary precepts.[112] Thus legal applications may not be the ultimate arbiter to resolve the many differences, but knowing the bases of these legal claims may better guide potential ways to manage multilateral disputes as they arise.[113] In large part, these legal disputes are how the contenders present their claims, so examining them this way is useful to illustrate the issues involved.

Customary International Laws and Claims.

Although by themselves the land features of the Spratly Islands have sustained no human population and produced little economically, they are points of contention because an island may garner legal jurisdiction and control over adjoining waters and resources.[114] To establish these benefits, a state uses customary, or traditional, international law to stake its claim through long association in a historic claim or discovery and occupation of a feature—each a separate mechanism to establish sovereignty but which some states employ together like overlapping insurance policies. Once sovereignty is determined, the type of feature owned dictates the forms of maritime jurisdictions that may then extend from it.[115] Customary law has evolved over the centuries, like common law, mainly from European traditions based on generally accepted notions, or past precedence through agreements, arbitration, or rulings by international courts. Concepts in customary law evolve as state practices change, and tend to address only specific issues presented within certain contexts. Among Asian societies Western customary legal concepts like sovereignty, the high seas, or coastal jurisdiction have no traditional equivalent which makes adjudicating ancient claims incongruent with modern procedures.[116] Socialist governments around the South China Sea also assert that "Bourgeois international law serves the interests of the bourgeoisie only," although they

21

employ these methods to advance their interests even as they seek to change them.[117] Customary law is also not codified and agreed upon in as rigorous a manner as UNCLOS, all of which leaves traditional law exceedingly complex and open to many interpretations and differences in its application.[118]

UNCLOS purposefully does not address sovereignty over land and "is premised on the assumption that a particular state has undisputed title over territory from which the maritime zone is claimed."[119] Thus customary law is the usual means to settle sovereignty disputes over territory through international law (of course other means exist like conquest or purchase), and its maritime customs are still sometimes invoked today as well. UNCLOS has indirectly spurred island claims since its negotiations began in the 1970s by assigning oceanic jurisdiction to nearly any land feature, thereby converting previously avoided desolate rock obstacles into the focal points of potential oceanic riches, and igniting a form of gold rush in the Spratly Islands. There are a few cases where territorial sovereignty claims are pressed through UNCLOS as well. Along with new technologies and rapidly expanding populations and economic needs, the new Law of the Sea Treaty explains why island disputes have turned more serious and violent in the South China Sea since the 1970s and why we study old legal principles to understand a 21st-century problem.[120]

Historic Vietnamese and Chinese Claims under Customary Law.

The oldest method of establishing jurisdiction over the features and waters of the South China Sea is to claim "historic rights," "historic waters," or "historic title" to them. In essence this concept states that an area has been part of a state, through long continuous administrative control, economic use, or social links, which should give the claimant special consideration for inherent usage rights in the area; or as its internal waters or sovereign territory when the claim is generally recognized by other states.[121] The appeal of maintaining a doctrine of historic claims comes from the legal principle of *stare decisis* ("maintain what has been decided," or settled law) offering the advantage of stability and continuity in law and governance, which is why it was accepted as a precept by the International Court of Justice in 1951.[122] In contrast, in traditional East Asian politics before Western legal concepts were practiced, a historic association of a region to a people or state would preclude the need for a formal legal claim to perennially oversee or control it.[123]

Although a practical customary precept, even in Western international law historic claims are broad and not well-defined traditionally or in the Law of the Sea Treaty.[124] Generally, historic rights recognize that traditional activities may continue in a designated area, or, if specifically stated, may also include a claim to a land area or maritime jurisdiction.[125] The concept of historic claims "over which a nation exercises sovereign authority," has been occasionally noted "under international law in limited situations," but the ambiguity of these concepts' wide ranging and sometimes conflicting interpretations mean they may not be useful mechanisms for establishing control.[126] Nonetheless, when such claims are made they are accompanied by detailed historic documentation to build a case in favor of the claimant which would then need to be verified and weighed against other conflicting claims. Such procedures favor cultures with long traditions in writing and record keeping. Using this mechanism to establish sovereignty or jurisdiction under modern practices requires that claims be backed by effective, continuous, and unchallenged occupation or administration to be valid.[127] These latter criteria are usually hard to establish, and thus may account in part for the past and present practice of challenging or ejecting nonsubject people from disputed areas in order to demonstrate some control over the claims,[128] resulting in some of the violent incidents this monograph has documented.

In the Spratly Islands region, there are two conflicting historic claims made by three parties: the PRC, ROC, and Vietnam, with the PRC and ROC sharing mutually supporting identical claims.[129] Vietnam presents a classic historic case for all of the Spratly and Paracel Islands, and an undelimitated amount of most of the South China Sea built on four historical arguments presented in three White Papers in 1979, 1982, and 1988.[130] As evidence, Vietnam presents historic records and maps showing it was the first state to discover and name the Spratlys, using court documents from as early as the reign of King Le Tanh Tong (1460-97), and "that the 'Feudal Vietnamese State' effectively controlled the two archipelagoes since the 17th century according to international law."[131] Vietnam also invokes the 1884 French claim and administration over the Spratlys while the Vietnamese states were a French protectorate and ultimate successor to their Western legal-style claim.[132] After it gained independence, a modern Vietnamese scholar could assert that:

> a long time ago, regional countries pursued their normal activities in the East Sea[133] without encountering any Chinese impediment and they have never recognized China's historic rights in the South China Sea. . . .[134]

24

More archival records are being translated into English to bolster Vietnam's historic claim to the entire region.[135]

The Vietnamese historic claim to any of the Spratly Islands tends to be inconclusive, however. Many non-Vietnamese scholars have found that basic Vietnamese knowledge about the Spratly Islands in its historic documents was weak and depended much on conveyed European misperceptions of the region.[136] When more accurate information about the Spratlys was attained by Vietnamese authorities "there is little evidence that the Nguyen dynasty [1802-1945] upheld its claim through declarations, effective occupation, or utilization."[137]

The Vietnamese claim has not been generally recognized, having been ignored in the 1951 peace conference in San Francisco in which Japan relinquished control of the islands after World War II; and the claim has been consistently protested and interfered with by other states since the 1950s.[138] Other telling blows were official statements by the Democratic Republic of Vietnam's (North Vietnam) Second Foreign Minister in 1956 and Prime Minister in 1958 that recognized the PRC's stated territorial claims which included both the Paracel and Spratly Islands, even while acknowledging disagreements over their land border. That same government today renounces the earlier support to PRC territorial claims as a necessity during their wars against foreigners,[139] but such recent recantations cannot help underscore a weak historic claim that is difficult to support.

The Chinese claim to the South China Sea and its geologic features is even more extensive than that of the Vietnamese,[140] but is just as ill-defined. Whether

China claims all of the sea and resources of the region, as indicated in terms officially used like "territorial waters"; just the Spratlys and other land features within the South China Sea, as may be intended with assertions to "historic title"; unspecified traditional rights in the region, like fishing, or some combination of these; they are voraciously defended as "historically belonging to China," and "China's intrinsic and inseparable territories" under the historic claim doctrine.[141] Chinese records show use of the sea that date to the Tang (618-907) and Song (960-1279) dynasties when a "Marine Silk Route" to Arabia and Africa developed.[142] Political oversight of the Spratly Islands may have started during the Yuan dynasty (1271-1368), and economic activities like fishing followed during the Ming dynasty (1368-1644).[143] Chinese association with the Spratlys is better documented from the mid-1800s through artifacts, trading records, refuge for nomadic fisherman, and diplomatic interactions with European powers or policing actions against them.[144] For instance, in 1876 China's ambassador to Great Britain declared the Paracel Islands as Chinese territory, and in 1883 the Chinese expelled a German survey team on the Spratly Islands.[145] To clarify its heretofore rather inconsistent claims against other powers in the South China Sea, a Chinese committee on land and water boundaries published a document in 1935 listing 96 land features above low tide level as Chinese territory.[146] In 1947, the ROC consolidated the Chinese historic claim by publishing a map with its "traditional maritime boundary line" (more often referred to as the "9-dashed line" or "U-shaped line," see Map 1) enclosing most of the South China Sea waters and associated land features as its "indisputable sovereignty."[147] The 1948 announcement that followed to explain the claim was purposely vague as to what was actually claimed , whether all the waters, just its land features, unspecified rights in the region like use of the sea bed, or some combination of these—an ambiguity that both Chinese governments have continued to maintain.[148] The Chinese claim their historic links to the Spratlys were well recognized until the 1930s when the French made claim to them through their then colonial possession of Tonkin (northern Vietnam), and the Japanese annexed them during World War II. In support, the Chinese cite an 1887 Sino-French treaty in which all islands east of a delimitation line belonged to China. Both the Spratly and Paracel Islands lie east of this line, although neither was specifically named, and the French would later contest that the treaty was a local agreement and not one of such wide scope.[149]

Despite Chinese documentation claiming the Spratlys, there are problems with its arguments because Chinese association with them has often lacked the clear consistent claims or effective administration required by modern international judgments.[150] Although not itself strong because it suffers from the same flaws, Vietnam's historic claim nonetheless contests China's assertions to acquiescence by other states and that it has been a victim of European imperial aggression. Vietnam, for instance, refuses to stamp new PRC passports bearing a map showing the South China Sea as part of China, and has opposed an annual May-to-August fishing ban in the South China Sea imposed by China.[151] Non-Chinese scholars also note that other competing claims for some or all of the Spratly islands have been made since the 1800s by France, Britain, and Japan, pushing China into asserting formal Western legal style sovereignty claims.[152] As already shown, more recent claims by the Philippines, Vietnam, Malaysia, and Brunei demonstrate that other states have not recognized China's claims, and China has not sufficiently maintained continuous or effective control.

Chinese counterarguments that its sovereignty over the Spratlys was strong until French incursions in the 1930s, are viewed dimly in light of inconsistent claims and the weak exercise of authority up to the end of World War II. For instance, an official Chinese report from 1928 delineates the Paracel Islands as China's southern border, and did not include the Spratly Islands.[153] During the 1943 Cairo Conference among the belligerents fighting Japan, attending ROC President Chiang Kai-shek made no claims for any Japanese occupied territory in the Spratlys, despite the fact that decisions about occupied lands was a main topic of the conference. As noted earlier, the ROC also withdrew troops landed there after World War II in 1950 and these were not replaced until 1956; and the PRC attempted no control of the islets until 1988. Also, during the 1951 negotiations over the peace treaty with Japan, 46 of 50 participating countries rejected a Soviet call to assign the Japanese conquered areas, including the Spratlys and Paracels, to the PRC.[154] A senior intelligence officer at the U.S. Pacific Fleet in a personal capacity challenged Chinese historic claims even further when he declared in 2013 that the claims were:

> the rubric of a maritime history that is not only contested in the international community but has largely been fabricated by Chinese government propaganda bureaus in order to . . . 'educate' the populace about China's rich maritime history.[155]

Chinese and Vietnamese officials have shown historic use of the southern South China Sea and its features but not to the level needed to establish effective control and thus sovereignty, since other states were also using and claiming parts of this area during these periods.[156] Some commentators believe China and Vietnam might have more success by converting their claims to one of historic rights to things like fishing, which are better documented historic activities by both in the region.[157] In short, the Chinese and Vietnamese historic claims for control over the Spratly Islands and their surrounding waters "can generally be summarized as incomplete, intermittent, and unconvincing."[158] Widely accepted international precedents, like the Island of Palmas Case ruled by the Permanent Court of Arbitration in 1925 and in subsequent cases,[159] find effective administration and occupation of land take precedence over first discovery, historic claims, or close proximity.[160] The Vietnamese and Chinese historic claims to the Spratly Islands lack a sufficient weight of evidence to establish the requirements of persistent effective control by their respective governments, sustainable population, or enduring economic activity with the Islands sufficient to clearly establish sovereignty or rights to specific activities.[161]

Sovereign Claims under the Customary Law of Discovery and Occupation.

More in accord with modern customary legal precepts, because it is centered on effective control, is the customary legal principle of discovery and occupation. China, Vietnam, the Philippines, and Malaysia have each staked out some or all of the Spratly Islands using this method. Like historic claims, which are increasingly being held to the same modern standard of effective administration, land stakes made through discovery and occupation require that a first claim be made for a land feature and then consistently and effectively controlled to remain valid.[162] This land must previously be *res nullis* ("nobody's property"),[163] and thus "discovered," and open for occupation and exploitation. More important is the "subsequent continuous and effective acts of occupation, generally construed to mean permanent settlement," although for uninhabitable islands that standard may be less strict but then garners fewer jurisdictional rights, as will be covered in the next section.[164] In the indeterminate nature of historic claim law, one could argue that historic claims fall under the doctrine of discovery and occupation through long-term association, although the difference in evidence presented, time frames, and inclusion of historic waters or rights may make them separate types of claims which are often how the parties to the Spratly Island disputes present them. In the South China Sea some formal discovery and occupation claims started in the 1800s, but many now cited originated after 1945 when defeated Japan renounced its World War II annexations leaving a void in ownership, and arguably resetting all the geologic features to *res nullis*. As examined below, each party derives its claim through discovery and occupation differently, but the evolving requirement for effective control and habitation accounts for the sudden interest in occupying the land features of the Spratly Islands (mainly through military garrisons so far) from which the occupying party would then seek to establish sovereignty over some or all of the islets.[165]

In addition to its historic claim, as well as supporting it, China also asserts that "Beijing has indisputable sovereignty over the islands based on discovery and prior occupation" as PRC President Yan Shang Kun declared in 1991.[166] Under its modern application, discovery and occupation of the Spratly Islands began in 1946 after ROC President Chiang Kai-shek ordered the occupation of Itu Aba and followed this with the publication of the infamous U-shaped line claim to the South China Sea.[167] Despite an interruption of its occupation from 1950-56 after losing the Chinese Civil War, Taiwan continued to assert its claim over the archipelago based on the 1952 Sino-Japanese Treaty which recognized Chinese sovereignty over the Spratlys. However, Japan had previously renounced all claims to the Spratlys, with no successor assigned, and the 1951 San Francisco Treaty refused to recognize any Spratly claims. Undeterred, Taiwan retorted that such actions could not nullify its sovereignty grounded on earlier historic claims and occupation.[168] Taiwan, for instance, extends its civilian control over Itu Aba as a municipality that is part of Kaohsiung's Cijin District, and it has its own postal code.[169] Bracketing the ROC's early single occupation are the much later occupations by the PRC to the same claims starting in 1988 when it established a physical PLA presence in the archipelago. This late occupation was preceded by much earlier discovery claims to all of the Spratlys by the PRC in 1951, and maritime rights from these features in 1958. Administrative control was furthered under PRC laws passed in 1992 and 1998 specifying Chinese maritime jurisdiction and rights,[170] and with the incorporation in July 2012 of Sansha, located on the Paracel's Woody Island, as the administrative prefecture-level city for all of its South China Sea claims including the Spratly Islands.[171] Physical possession of its seven features is crucial to supporting its claim, as demonstrated when the Philippines vacated and subsequently lost Mischief Reef to PLA occupation in 1995 as part of China's final acquisition in the Spratlys.[172]

Just as the shared PRC and ROC historic claim has been vigorously contested, so too have their discovery and occupation claims for many of the same reasons. After World War II, France also sent an expedition to the Spratlys to contest the Chinese occupation and re-establish its claims, although the French did not leave a physical presence.[173] Not only have Chinese claims to the Spratlys been contested by other states since they were first made under discovery and occupation, but its interrupted and limited control over the islands have not supported China's extensive claims. Taiwan occupies only Itu Aba as its sole garrison in the Sprat-lys (and for 12 years the only one among all the dis-putants). It did so based on its understanding of cus-tomary law that, by occupying the major land feature in a group, control over the other associated features was assumed.[174] This practice has not been honored by the other parties. The PRC's administrative control activities only started during the 1970s followed by its first physical occupation after all other claimants.[175] The PRC delayed its opportunity for effective control while turned inward during divisive political move-ments and modernization, allowing Vietnam, the Philippines, and Malaysia a 30-year lead in discovery and effective occupation through permanent outposts and structures built on previously vacant Spratly fea-tures.[176] Chinese actions have been routinely disputed by other states, such as when Sansha City was estab-lished incorporating all of its South China Sea claims into the PRC's municipal system, with Vietnam and the Philippines expectedly protesting but so did, un-usually, the United States.[177] Aggressive PRC actions in the South China Sea since the Sansha City disputes may in part be to make up for the appearance of weak administration over the Spratlys by asserting control through more enforcement of its national laws to show it sufficiently governs them as part of its jurisdiction.

Since Vietnam's historic claim to the Spratly Islands is no stronger than China's longer and more documented evidence, Vietnamese officials have instead gradually emphasized the principle of discovery and occupation claiming that the archipelago was *res nullis* before 1933. In reality, the original claim began in 1884 when France established a protectorate over Vietnam along with both the Paracel and Spratly Islands.[178] In 1930, wary of Japanese expansion in East Asia, France consummated its earlier discovery by annexing Spratly Island and 3 years later claimed all of the Spratleys and occupied, for the first time, nine islets until they were, in turn, occupied by Japan between 1937 and 1938.[179] As the legal successor to French claims based from the Vietnamese protectorate, Vietnam asserts it subsequently assumed this claim to the Spratlys when it gained divided independence in 1954.[180] However, South Vietnamese attempts at effective administration followed much later in 1974 when the Spratlys were incorporated into Vietnam's Phuoc Tuy province, and off-shore oil exploration contracts were let.[181] In 1975, North Vietnam took control of South Vietnam's recently established Spratly garrisons and claim (along with the rest of the country), and placed additional forces on other features, growing from 13 to 21 positions by 1997 and to 29 garrisons today.[182] To assert its control, Vietnam has since established Spratly Island as a township in Truòng Sa district, organized local elections and tours in the Spratlys, and has continued to award oil exploration contracts.[183] Vietnam's claims to the Spratlys were formally delimitated in a maritime law passed by the National Assembly in June 2012.[184]

These acquired claims are difficult to substantiate since the Chinese have routinely challenged all French and Vietnamese claims in the area, and, as noted earlier, North Vietnamese authorities during the 1950s officially supported the PRC claim to the Spratlys.[185] Also, neither France nor the then semi-independent Vietnam pressed their claim during the 6 years from 1950 to 1956 when the Spratlys were entirely unoccupied — in part because both turned inward to address more pressing domestic troubles and wished to remain in good standing with China.[186] Further condemning the Vietnamese claim is that France asserts that it made its claims to the Spratlys for itself rather than in the name of Vietnam.[187] In 1950, responsibility for the defense of the Paracel Islands was transferred by the French to the Vietnamese, with subsequent Vietnamese licensed economic activity ensuing in the form of phosphate mining.[188] However, no such turnover occurred with the Spratlys, and in 1956 both Vietnam and France delivered separate protests to the Philippines government when citizens from that country claimed parts of the Spratlys. However, in 1957 the French allowed its Spratly Islands claim to go passive, neither relinquishing nor defending its claim, leaving the Vietnamese inherited claim in limbo.[189] Since then, the PRC, ROC, Malaysia, the Philippines, and Brunei all have routinely contested the extensive Vietnamese claims to most of the South China Sea in words and deeds of their own. Despite its historic documentation, assertions of discovery, and assumption of French claims, Vietnam's stark physical possession of the many features in the Spratlys seems to be its strongest claim to the region

With no historic claim of its own, the Philippines relies on the principle of discovery and occupation, and their close proximity, to claim nearly all of the Spratly Islands, except Spratly Island itself and other points west of it.[190] Filipino involvement in the Spratlys was spurred by a private entrepreneur, Tomas Cloma, who by 1950 established several colonies on the islets to open a fish cannery and exploit guano deposits.[191] With no official government action following, Cloma, with his brother Filemon and encouragement from the Philippine Vice President, formally claimed this region as his own in 1956, and named it Kalaya'an (Freedomland).[192] Although these actions alarmed the ROC government, which rushed to re-establish its military presence on Itu Aba, the Philippines government only officially occupied five features in the nearby Reed Bank area in 1971 after the prospects for discovering oil were apparent. In 1978, the Philippines occupied two more islets in the Spratlys, and formally claimed the Kalaya'an Group, and incorporated it into Palawan province, through Presidential Decree Number 1596.[193] The Philippines government also based its discovery and occupation on the features being *res nullis* and open to occupation after World War II. They interpret all earlier historic and occupation claims to the Spratlys as void because based on the 1951 San Francisco Treaty the island group was "de facto under the trusteeship of the Allied Powers" and thus "as 'trusts' nullified any previous ownership of them. . . ."[194] With a clean slate, military occupation, and active economic exploitation through fishing and drilling for energy (even if no sustained economic activity on the islets themselves), the Philippines government has staked its claim to Kalaya'an through discovery and effective occupation.

The Philippines' stake in the Spratlys is, of course, hotly disputed by other claimants. The Philippines makes no historic claim to the Spratlys because the Spanish-American treaty of 1898, which transferred possession of the Philippines to the United States, explicitly established a western limit that excluded the Spratlys. Upon Philippine independence in 1946, American advisors discouraged Filipino claims to the Spratlys based upon this treaty and to avoid conflict with the ROC, a wartime ally.[195] When Tomas Cloma took private ownership of the islands in 1956, the ROC, France, and independent South Vietnam protested this action to the Philippine government.[196] Each disputed that their previous claims were not abandoned or null, and instead found Cloma's claim invalid since a private citizen may not claim land unless acting on behalf of a sovereign state, and the Philippines government did not sanction his actions. As further evidence, the Philippines did not include the nearby Kalaya'an area within its straight line baselines that officially declared the extent of the Philippine archipelago in 1955.[197] Contiguous proximity to the Spratlys, as the closest state adjacent to many of the Spratly features, also does not strengthen the Filipino claim, since the 1925 *Island of Palmas* and subsequent cases established effective occupation as the standard for possession — not distance.[198] The Philippines also waited 25 years after they claimed the islands reverted to *res nullis* before discovering and occupying any of them. Thus, the Philippine claim is no stronger than the others, and suffers from having no supporting claim through historic or proximity arguments.

As Vietnam's discovery and occupation claim to its protector's much earlier discovery was undercut by subsequent French action, a potential Malaysian succession to an early discovery in the Spratlys was also undercut by the British — forcing Malaysia to make a separate and later claim of its own. The British were probably the first Europeans to land in the Spratlys, and the archipelago is named after a British sailor.[199] The first documented Western legal claim to the Spratlys was made in 1877 for Spratly Island and Amboyna Cay by Britain based from its Labuan Crown Colony in Borneo. During the 1880s, Britain's Central Borneo Company planned to gather guano commercially from these islets, but operations may not have followed.[200] These islets were included on the British Colonial Office List, although little more was done to perfect the claim.[201] In 1933, when the French pursued their Spratly claim more vigorously, the British allowed its claim to go dormant, neither abandoning its own discovery nor challenging the claims of others.[202] Thus Malaysia had to make its own discovery and occupation claim after acquiring the northern Borneo states from Britain in 1963. Malaysia's discovery began in 1979 with the official publication of a map claiming 12 Spratly features, with occupation following in 1983 at Swallow Reef and subsequently four other features.[203]

Malaysia's claims are also contested in full by China, and in part by the Philippines and Vietnam. In fact, Amboyna Cay, for which the British made a claim in 1877, is currently occupied by Vietnamese forces, and thus Malaysia has not demonstrated effective control over its claim.[204] Malaysia has resolved its overlapping differences in the South China Sea with the enclave country of Brunei, however.[205] Of all the claimants, Malaysian diplomats are most effective at reasonably resolving disputes. They have established model agreements and bilateral joint development zones with both Vietnam and Thailand in disputed waters near peninsular Malaysia, and have submitted a joint continental shelf claim in the South China Sea with Vietnam.[206] Nor does Malaysia claim all features and waters that it could if it pressed its maritime stake to a line equidistant from its national shores meeting in the middle similar claims for the Spratly Islands drawn for other states. Malaysia also resolved its South China Sea differences with Indonesia centered on Natuna Basar by defining the two maritime borders for peninsular and insular Malaysia. The Indonesian agreement may have set a bad precedent for other Malaysian claims, however, since it accepted less control over the disputed continental shelf than allowed under UNCLOS, with some commentators concluding that in such moderate actions "Malaysia has undercut its own potential claim to some extent. . . ."[207]

Under customary sovereignty law, historic ownership principles made by Vietnam and China are generally thought to be weak, and discovery and occupation is fiercely contested, although effectively executed, given the myriad examples cited here.[208] Employing traditional methods of establishing sovereignty over the Spratlys has justified assertive actions that have created tension and frustration, and at worst precarious standoffs and pitched battles that have killed.[209] Because of these sometimes violent disputes, the potential riches of the South China Sea are squandered through uncoordinated nonsustainable overuse in the case of fishing, or nonuse through lack of investment and development due to unstable political conditions in the case of hydrocarbon energy. The Spratly Islands have become a literal patchwork of intermingled seizures and occupations rendering confusing and overlapping potential maritime jurisdictions. Perhaps it is not surprising that the customary law used by European states to build and fight over empires in North America, the Middle East, South Asia, and Southeast Asia would also lead to tension when applied in the South China Sea. With the economic, political, and emotional issues involved, it may be highly unlikely to reverse the many resulting physical military occupations in the Spratlys, and "very difficult, if not impossible, for China to negotiate the 'return' of those islands" as Dr. Lai observes.[210]

These fixed positions of sovereignty may be a solution, although a messy one, to possession and exploitation of the Spratly Islands through adapting another Roman based international customary law, *uti possidetis* ("as you possess, thus may you possess"). This principle allows a party to maintain as its property its current possession until its rightful owner is ascertained. In international law, that is interpreted to mean land gained (often in war) remains with the occupier unless otherwise disposed through a treaty. This principle was upheld by the International Court of Justice in 1986 when it ruled to maintain the colonial borders inherited by independent states in the case *Burkina Faso vs. Mali*.[211] This law could apply to the Spratly Islands if the claimants kept their present possessions, under whatever method they were gained, unless a subsequent formal settlement is negotiated. However, this arrangement could lead to disputes and violence as the many yet unprocessed features, rocks, reefs and even underwater geologic protrusions, are snatched and occupied in a new "land rush" melee. This is an expensive and dangerous solution fraught with many perils of which the claimants should be wary, especially since not all parties may continue to adhere to the present consensus that garrisons in place remain undisturbed. Further conflict for possessions thus could occur following the lead of the great European imperial powers, with the strongest imposing its will on the others.

United Nations Convention on the Law of the Sea and Spratly Claims.

Should the problem of sovereignty over each or all of the Spratly Islands be resolved, the issue of what is gained in the maritime realm through their possession is the province of UNCLOS. The U.S. position on this issue was revealed by then Secretary of State Hillary Clinton in 2010 at the ARF:

> We believe claimants should pursue their territorial claims and accompanying rights to maritime space in accordance with the UN Convention on the Law of the Sea. Consistent with customary international law, legitimate claims to maritime space in the South China Sea should be derived solely from legitimate claims to land features.[212]

The issue of sovereignty is so central that some South China Sea claimants argue for the possession of land features using UNCLOS, although that is explicitly not its stated purpose. Land claims through UNCLOS are sometimes made when other claims through customary law seem weak or because of the perception that claims made through UNCLOS may have higher standing in the eyes of the international community. Because of the importance of UNCLOS, this section discusses its key points that affect the Spratly region dispute, including how maritime jurisdiction is determined when originating from a land feature, the different maritime zones and their rights, and the sea and land claims that the South China Sea disputants have lodged using these rules.

Well-defined maritime boundaries and agreed upon rights within them are necessary to peace and stability on the ocean commons.[213] Customary maritime law, through most of history, governed space, and actions on the seas by allocating 3-mile-wide territorial waters from a coast, with general agreement on rights for navigation and taking of resources. Since the 1950s, however, management of the sea has become much more regulated and comprehensive through a series of international treaties culminating in UNCLOS (also known as the Law of the Sea Treaty), which was negotiated from 1973 to 1982 and took effect in 1994. This treaty gives coastal states a 12-nm territorial sea, and an exclusive economic zone (EEZ) of limited economic control to 200-nm from the coast, and possibly a continental shelf extension to the natural limit of its seabed shelf (to a maximum of 350-nm). It also has provisions for archipelagic states to enclose the waters around and between their islands as internal waters giving more economic and security control within their physically fragmented countries.[214] These maritime boundaries of state control are premised on the type of land feature each emanates from (inhabitable land or unproductive rock), so that the issues of sovereignty, topography, and classification of a land feature determines maritime boundaries.[215]

Each of the states claiming the Spratlys has ratified this convention, although often with reservations. Taiwan, however, is not eligible to be a member, although it generally follows its rules, and the United States has signed but not ratified the treaty.[216] Technically, UNCLOS does not apply to disputes started before it came into effect, including all of the Spratly claims, but an expectation exists for signatories to abide by its provisions nonetheless.[217] Four forms of settlement are offered by UNCLOS for dispute resolution, with arbitration the assumed form since none of the states involved have yet chosen a method. States are able to

opt out of some of the Law of the Sea Treaty's requirements. The PRC and the other claimant states, for instance, do not accept compulsory procedures to settle
disputes over maritime boundaries, military or legal
activities in a zone, or actions of the Security Council,
because those provisions might interfere with the dis-
cretionary sovereign powers of the state.[218] Thus UN-
CLOS is a well-respected treaty that offers guidance to
resolve disputes like those found in the South China
Sea, but rarely does so through strict enforcement.[219]

Determination of a Habitable Island from a Rock.

After designating sovereignty over a land feature,
which is normally deemed beyond the pale of UN-
CLOS, determining the type of feature from which a
maritime zone is claimed is the next step and one of
the functions of the law of the sea. Inhabitable lands
receive full consideration of all UNCLOS maritime
zones and rights, although these can be constrained
by surrounding zones. Continental states receive this
full consideration for territorial waters and adjacent
EEZ or continental shelf, while islands may be assigned some or all of those areas.[220] However, what
constitutes an inhabitable island is a major concern
since a qualified speck of land could accrue control
over 125,000 nm^2 of water column and seabed through
the UNCLOS regime. Under Article 121:

> an island is a naturally formed area of land, surround-
> ed by water, which is above water at high tide [,but] . . .
> Rocks which cannot sustain human habitation or
> economic life of their own shall have no exclusive
> economic zone or continental shelf.[221]

The human considerations in the island definition establishes a sub-class of islands known as "rocks" which are "barren and uninhabitable insular formations, such as cays and atolls," and receive only territorial waters and a contiguous zone around them regardless of the size of the rocks.[222]

Respected Spratly Island experts Mark Valencia, Jon Van Dyke, and Noel Ludwig have determined that 25 to 35 features in the region "are above water at high tide, and these qualify as islands . . . and appear to be entitled to territorial seas."[223] They also note, per Article 121, that reefs and other features submerged at high tide garner no maritime zones "even if artificial structures are based on them," except for a 500-meter safety zone given to any artificial or temporary feature at sea.[224] Under these terms, some of the PRC's current Spratly occupations might garner no maritime zones since they are perched upon submerged reefs, which may also pertain to some of the other countries' occupations like Malaysia's Swallow Reef, Vietnam's Barque Canada Reef, and the Philippine's Commodore Reef.[225] In 1975, the International Court of Justice advised that the standard for formal displays of sovereignty, like markers and policing, are lower for uninhabited areas, which would also pertain to islands designated as rocks.[226] This monograph has deliberately not used the word "island" indiscriminately, in order to accurately distinguish features as used by these various definitions.

Because the stakes are high for how a maritime land feature is designated and the definitions used in UNCLOS are not precise, leeway is often employed to interpret this clause. Whereas physical geography may distinguish between an island and a nonisland geologic feature, human needs distinguish between a habitable island and a rock. The key question then is, "What does it take to sustain human habitation or have economic life of its own?"[227] A source of indigenous potable water might be one criterion, but would that prevent a solar powered desalinization plant from also fulfilling the requirement for "human habitation . . . on their own?" Must the island itself sustain its population with the necessities of life to be habitable, or may it be supplied from outside? Are lighthouses or navigation markers sufficient evidence of "economic life of their own"?[228] Van Dyke has argued cogently that a habitable island requires a permanent sustainable population "who are on the land area for reasons other than just to secure a claim of a distant population for the adjacent ocean resources." He explicitly discounts occupation forces and lighthouse keepers from this group.[229] He further believes, with other experts, that a population of at least 50 people could constitute a sufficiently stable community to satisfy the habitation requirement, although he has conceded:

> The criterion may not inevitably require that the insular feature itself be permanently inhabited, but it would require, at a minimum, that it provide support for a regular basis by fisheries from neighboring islands. . . .[230]

The indeterminate nature of the habitable criterion leaves much room for the claimants and experts to argue and disagree.

Under some circumstances, rocks and inhabited islands may not receive full maritime zones.[231] Rocks receive little consideration under international law to prevent them from impinging on similar rights of nearby islands or continents that are populous and economically active, to not interfere with opportunities that should be open to all seafaring nations when located on the high seas, and to reduce the incentive to "reverse engineer" a barren feature with a settlement that could claim a maritime zone that would make the feature economically viable when it was not originally.[232] Even habitable islands hold lesser status under UNCLOS when compared against the claims of a continental coast. In the 1984 International Court of Justice case between Libya and Malta, the latter was given:

> a diminished capacity to generate maritime zones in comparison to the broad coastline of Libya . . . thus even substantial and heavily populated islands are not the equivalent of continental landmasses in their ability to support claims over adjacent ocean space.[233]

Another example of a similar application pertinent to the Spratly Islands is that uninhabitable islands generating territorial waters would not impede the rest of the rights attributed to a larger maritime zone, like an EEZ, that may encompass it.[234] This would apply, for instance, to Mischief Reef which, if it were found to at least meet the status of a rock, would generate territorial waters for the PRC within the Philippine's EEZ, and with Amboyna Cay for Vietnam's occupation within Malaysia's EEZ. The vague considerations that are taken into account in determining maritime boundaries and the other short comings of UNCLOS means that most dispute settlements tend to be difficult, and usually considered on a case-by-case basis using precedent only as a guide if submitted for review.[235]

Questioning their habitability, the Spratly Islands' conditions prove harsh for personnel living there, as one Chinese newspaper recorded that soldiers must endure "shortages of fresh water and vegetables, loneliness, bad weather, and hard life. . . ."[236] The resulting cost of the financial and physical commitment by each occupying state is high,[237] and may explain in part why the Philippines withdrew from Mischief Reef in 1995, allowing PLAN troops to occupy the feature in their stead. The nearest case of a disputed South China Sea feature meeting the requirements for a habitable island may be Woody Island, the largest of the Paracels, occupied and settled by the PRC with a decades-old population of some size.[238] To demonstrate its control and habitability of this island, the PRC has made it an administrative capital and significantly upgraded its transportation and life support infrastructure.[239] Itu Aba, occupied by Taiwan and the largest island in the Spratlys group, is reported to have two natural springs on the island, but has never had a permanent population nor sustained economic activity on its own, despite many attempts to show official control.[240] Hasjim Djalal, an Indonesian expert who was President of the UNCLOS Assembly of the International Sea-Bed Authority and coordinator of the informal "Track II" workshops among the South China Sea disputants, doubts that any of the Spratly Islands could be considered habitable.[241] In 2009 when establishing continental shelf claims with the UN, Vietnam and Malaysia made no shelf claims based on contested islands, indicating they did not meet Article 121 viability or economic criteria to do so. The new principles and definitions in the 1982 UNCLOS law have stirred problems in the South China Sea, which some commentators believe could best be managed by declaring the features "legally uninhabitable,"[242] or pooling the maritime zones each might generate to be "shared regionally and managed by a joint development resource agency."[243] Within these bookends of open ocean and collective sovereign waters lays a continuum of maritime control by the coastal states.

Maritime Jurisdictions.

After sovereignty over a geologic feature and its type are determined, then the maritime jurisdictions it controls are established through UNCLOS. The Law of the Sea Treaty determines how much authority a state asserts over neighboring sea as weighted by the type of land feature it is based upon and the distance from the coastline. The types of waters that may be assigned are sovereign internal waters (including closely related archipelagic and historic waters), territorial waters, contiguous zones, EEZs, sometimes a continental shelf extension, and the high seas. The high seas are the *res communis* open for use by all states, although regulated somewhat by both customary law and UNCLOS as to how activities may be conducted. Examples of regulating the high seas include customary laws against piracy or slavery, and UNCLOS Part XI rules on the gathering of nonliving and sedentary resources from the ocean floor[244] — objections to the latter has kept the United States from ratifying the Law of the Sea Treaty. The boundaries and rights of the littoral zones are explained in this section in order to better present the potential maritime jurisdictions that are claimed in the Spratly Islands region, and their implications for U.S. interests.

Internal, Archipelagic, and Historic Sovereign Waters.

The most restrictive maritime zones are internal waters in which the state has complete sovereignty, as if over its own internal lakes and land. Internal waters are adjacent national waters with access to the sea, but are inside a series of straight baselines that may connect barrier islands or cross the mouth of a narrow bay, and thus are treated as under the full sovereignty of the state.[245] Smooth coastline states might rate no internal waters, whereas countries with chains of nearby fringe islands, like the U.S. eastern seaboard, or deeply indented coastline, like that found in Alaska, would have internal waters from the shore to the straight baseline that connects the outer most part of these features, as stipulated in Article 7 and subsequent guidance in UNCLOS.[246] Applying this law, the United States has sovereign control over its Intracoastal Waterway on the landward side of the east coast barrier islands, but only territorial waters control on the seaward side of those islands. Establishing a straight baseline simplifies rugged sea borders, and is advantageous since it not only grants sovereign control over adjacent waters, but, as its name implies, moves the line from which other maritime zones are measured from the shore (or normal baseline) to the straight baseline, and makes all waters landward from the straight baseline sovereign internal waters. For this reason, straight baselines are often liberally drawn, as have been done by the PRC, Malaysia, the Philippines, and Vietnam, and which have been protested by the United States as exceeding their rightful allowances.[247] The only exception in UNCLOS to complete sovereignty over internal waters is to allow innocent passage across recently drawn straight baselines "which had not previously been considered as such," mostly affecting states through whose waters traditional international shipping routes pass.[248] Although straight baselines are not directly applied in the Spratly Islands, their use along neighboring shores does influence the amount of maritime jurisdiction that may be claimed among them from national boundaries.

A new construct for internal waters found in UNCLOS Part IV is that of archipelagic waters, codified in part to supersede the thorny concept of historic waters.[249] Archipelagic waters were specifically intended to give fragmented island states, like Indonesia and the Philippines, authority over the waters within the confines of their archipelago as defined by its baselines.[250] Here, however, the enclosing lines are called straight archipelagic baselines, and are drawn further afield than the tips of adjacent craggy peninsulas and fringe islands. Archipelagic baselines may connect the outermost features of an archipelago with lines up to 100-nm long to enclose an area of no more than 1 to 9 land to water ratio.[251] Although the Spratly Islands themselves are a geographic archipelago, they would not fall under this legal regime because they are not a sovereign state. Should the PRC or another continental state gain control over the Spratlys it could not control them through the archipelagic state provisions since the mainland is not a part of the archipelago.[252]

The Philippines, however, could be an exception since it is an archipelagic state as defined in 1961 in its *Republic Act 3046*, but which did not include the Spratlys among its homeland islands.[253] Australian geographer Dr. Victor Prescott, however, postulated that the Philippines could claim Kalaya'an as an archipelagic appendage in a scheme using three archipelagic baselines between 100 and 125-nm and drying reefs, both of which are explicitly allowed under UNCLOS Article 47. This new configuration would also keep an acceptable land to water ratio of 1:2.4. [254] In 2009, the Philippine Congress updated its maritime borders in the *Archipelagic Baseline Law of the Philippines* to better comply with international law. Although this act claims both Kalaya'an and nearby Scarborough Shoal as Philippine, it did not do so through archipelagic baselines despite much debate in support of using that method.[255] Thus, the Philippines claims the Spratlys through the island regime methods previously discussed, rather than these archipelagic procedures—although the new Philippine baseline law specifically does not rule out this method in the future, but declares it would only do so in full compliance with UNCLOS stipulations.[256]

Historic claims, beyond those now covered under archipelagic baseline rules, are also considered internal waters under customary law. Although historic waters are not officially defined, they are occasionally referenced in UNCLOS, such as Article 10's "historic bays" or Article 15's reference to "historic title."[257] According to maritime law author L. J. ɔouchez, historic waters are:

> waters over which the coastal State, contrary to the generally applicable rules of international law, clearly, effectively, continuously, and over a substantial period of time, exercises sovereign rights with the acquiescence of the community of States.[258]

Its appeal to states is that historic waters hold the sovereignty of internal waters, but do not include the innocent-transit-across-baselines caveat found in UNCLOS archipelagic waters regime. Thus attaining historic waters status restricts freedom of navigation and curtails the exploitation of oceanic resources by the international community.[259] As preceding law, historic waters may also override UNCLOS statutes, for instance allowing historic bays wider than 24-nm at the mouth, or giving precedence to historic waters contrary to overlapping territorial water claims which would otherwise be settled with a median line between them.[260] The motivation for a state to claim such waters is obvious, and both Vietnam and China make sweeping historic claims to large parts of the South China Sea, as previously presented.

Although some commentators assert that historic claim doctrine is obsolete or at least transitional, these claims remain very active in practice through the legal principle of *stare decisis*.[261] Nonetheless, UNCLOS was written to minimize the use of historic claims, and they are generally recognized by the international community only in exceptional circumstances.[262] As already demonstrated in the Spratlys, the Vietnamese and Chinese historic claims are not convincingly documented, lacking the continuity and long-term exercise of rights recognized by other states as defined by Bouchez. For example, it would be difficult for a state to claim historic waters where foreign ships transit on a regular basis as has routinely occurred around the Spratly Islands in the South China Sea.[263] Some officials in Beijing are reported to recognize that their sweeping claim for South China Sea historic waters conflicts with UNCLOS, and believe a more appropriate claim is for just the islets within its U-shaped line with their adjacent waters.[264] At least one commentator believes that Vietnamese officials are also relenting on claiming historic waters to argue its claims in terms of UNCLOS EEZ and continental shelf articles.[265] Although not taken seriously by the international community, historic waters could be a powerful and excluding disruptor if awarded to any claimant in the South China Sea.

Territorial Seas and Contiguous Zones.

Close to internal waters in concept and proximity are the maritime zones of territorial sea and contiguous waters. Territorial seas codify the customary legal practice of state control over waters within 3-nm of its shores, but UNCLOS expands this zone to up to 12-nm from the baseline. Articles 33 and 121 allow every natural feature above the high water mark to have territorial waters and up to an additional 12-nm for a contiguous zone, and each of the South China Sea states have established each of the UNCLOS allowed zones.[266] Territorial seas are treated as the coastal state's sovereign territory, with exclusive rights to living and nonliving resources down to and including the seabed and enforcement of applicable national laws, but must still allow innocent passage to transiting foreign vessels.[267] The right of innocent passage through territorial waters requires that "the peace, good order, or security of the coastal State" not be disturbed through activities like fishing, polluting, information collection, firing weapons, or launching aircraft or boats in accordance with Article 19.[268] Coastal states may, of course, prevent noninnocent passage through their territorial waters, and may also temporarily suspend innocent passage by all foreign vessels in specific areas as temporary security zones in their territorial sea per Article 25.[269] The contiguous zone is a nonsovereign transitional area that allows protections for the coastal state to enforce national laws concerning customs, finance, immigration, and sanitation, but is otherwise governed as part of the less restrictive EEZ.[270] Innocent passage is not needed to transit a contiguous zone. Both zones were established to allow freedom of navigation to all vessels from any state, but also to ensure good order and control over adjacent waters for the coastal state.

There are disagreements, however, over whether innocent passage applies to all vessels or excludes warships of another state, a major concern for the United States which relies on innocent passage for power projection. The 1958 convention that preceded UNCLOS clearly allowed warships innocent passage through territorial waters, and the drafting history of UNCLOS indicates the same rights.[271] UNCLOS rules for innocent passage fall under Section 3, Subsection A, entitled "Rules Applicable to All Ships" which states "ships of all States, whether coastal or land-locked, enjoy the right of innocent passage through the territorial sea."[272] Despite this rule, China, Vietnam, Malaysia and, in the past, the Philippines have interpreted innocent passage to exclude warships or their activities, and protest such transit vigorously.[273] Vietnam's 1980 *Enactment No. 30-CP* prohibits military ships from both its territorial sea and contiguous zone without 30 days advance permission, although its 2012 *Law of the Sea* has relaxed the requirement to just prior notification.[274] Further to sea are the PRC's permanent restricted maritime military zones, created in the 1960s, within and outside territorial waters in the Bo Hai and Yellow Sea.[275] Although these zones are north of the South China Sea, they demonstrate long-standing Chinese actions that ignore UNCLOS Article 25, and could also be applied around the claimed Spratly Islands as permanent political obstructions to any foreign vessel's passage in the region.

Chinese policy since the early days of the Republic in the 1920s, after its harsh history with maritime insecurity, also bars warships' passage through its territorial seas and contiguous zones without prior consent "to safeguard its national security."[276] This was first codified in the *Declaration of the Government of the PRC on the Territorial Sea* in 1958, and reiterated in the 1992 *Law on Territorial Waters and their Contiguous Areas*, both of which explicitly included the Paracel and Spratly Islands.[277] The significance of maritime control and innocent passage for the PRC explains in part why China took more than 13 years to ratify UNCLOS, and the reason for its accompanying reservations.[278] The issues of sovereignty and independence are the PRC's highest priority in its policy of *Five Principles of Peaceful Coexistence*. The 1992 territorial waters law implied, and actions have shown, that the PRC will enforce its sovereignty for its claimed Paracel and Spratly Islands.[279] Should this be fully enforced the international community would face sovereign zones carved out of the Spratly Islands region if the principle of discovery and occupation is applied, and could mean most or all of the sea becoming off limits without consent should China or Vietnam enforce historic rights to the islets or to historic waters.

Exclusive Economic Zones.

An innovation of modern maritime statutory law is the EEZ, by which states possessing habitable islands and continental shores economically control up to 200-nm of ocean and seabed from their baseline under Part V of UNCLOS.[280] Unlike territorial seas, however, there is no state sovereignty over this zone, just the authority to regulate the environment and natural resources, establishment of installations, and conduct of "marine scientific research."[281] By controlling such activities, EEZs are distinguished from the less-restrictive high seas. Unlike territorial seas, navigation and over flight of an EEZ is not subject to the coastal state's control except to enforce the authorities allowed by UNCLOS, such as resource management and pollution control.[282] Based on these provisions to manage the EEZ, the South China Sea states often challenge each other's activities in their ambiguous and overlapping claimed EEZs, and use their interpretations to restrict operations of foreign military craft—as already presented in this monograph.

Under customary law the distances over which states controlled adjacent waters were short, and the amount of overlapping jurisdictions small. When UNCLOS extended the maritime jurisdictions and created the EEZ, with states 400-nm apart becoming maritime neighbors, the problem of many unilateral and overlapping EEZ claims in the Spratlys resulted.[283] In such cases, delimitation establishes maritime jurisdiction boundaries between states' valid claims for territorial seas, contiguous zones, EEZs, and continental shelf.[284] To remove contention from such decisions the earlier *1958 Geneva Conventions on the Law of the Sea* proposed a line halfway between the coastlines of overlapping jurisdictions, using the "equidistance principle," to delimitate disputed areas that could not be otherwise settled.[285] However, this straightforward method was modified in the 1970s in international court judgments that found even habitable lands may each carry different weight in the generation of maritime zones based on the length of their coastlines.[286] Of course, where no overlap occurs, all habitable islands receive full maritime zones, but when small islands' jurisdictions abut larger islands or larger islands' zones overlap continental landmasses, the smaller feature will receive less than full effect depending on each circumstance.[287] Weighing the amount of jurisdiction awarded in disputes to the more significant land formation is the essence of the current "equitable principle," which ensures the amount of area awarded in an EEZ is proportional to the length of the coastlines involved, and not usually influenced by economic, ecological, or other characteristics.[288]

The awarding of an EEZ using these rules is important in the Spratly Islands because of the consequences for regional economic development and international navigation. Unlike territorial seas and contiguous zones, economically unviable rocks do not generate an EEZ or a continental shelf claim.[289] Under these conditions, an exposed rock would then become an enclave of territorial waters for one state surrounded by the high seas or the EEZ of another state's nearby eligible landmass.[290] Since the Philippines, Malaysia, Vietnam, and Brunei all claim 200-nm EEZs from their baselines, the states closest to the Spratlys would dominate the region's maritime resources, outside of the territorial waters given to some rocks. Thus Malaysia's EEZ would regulate the seas around the southeastern Spratly Islands; the Philippines, the seas around the northeastern features; Vietnam, the waters out to a few of the western most features (such as Spratly Island, West Reef, and parts of Rifleman Bank); and Brunei's EEZ would control around Louisa Reef.[291] Since Vietnam, Malaysia, and the Philippines have each also determined that none of their Spratly Islands are habitable in their EEZ and continental shelf submissions in 2009 to the UN Commission on the Limits of the Continental Shelf, none of the islands may generate an EEZ in their judgment.[292] This leaves a band of high seas stretching from the Northeast Cay to parts of Rifleman Bank in the southwestern Spratlys which would be governed only by UNCLOS Article 87, the Freedom of the High Seas section, and the International Seabed Authority for sea floor resources.[293] Where overlap occurs between their EEZs, Malaysia has shown a proclivity to delimitate its differences through diplomacy with Vietnam and Brunei in their joint EEZ and continental shelf claims — both accomplished in 2009.[294] When interpreted under the intent of UNCLOS, establishment of EEZs is relatively straightforward in the Spratlys' region.

Some aspects of EEZ claims in the South China Sea, however, are nonstandard or ambiguous, and their vigorous pursuit complicates the region's maritime delimitation. For instance, Brunei uses its 200-nm EEZ to claim Louisa Reef, with two small rocks above high tide, and then claims an EEZ around those rocks extending it to an equidistant line with Vietnam's zone that puts Rifleman Bank in Brunei's super-extended EEZ. Such a claim is probably not sustainable, however, since effective occupation, not UNCLOS, is the method to claim Louisa Reef, and Brunei has not done so nor enforced its maritime laws effectively in the EEZ. Furthermore, rocks cannot generate an EEZ on their own.[295] A different EEZ complication comes with the possibility of the Philippine's annexing the Spratlys as integral to its archipelago. In 1978, President Ferdinand Marcos proclaimed Kalaya'an as part of the Philippines and established an EEZ around all the Philippine Islands — which some commentators believe included the Spratlys — which could give the Philippines an additional baseline to establish an EEZ.[296] Although the Philippine government has not yet employed the archipelagic rules to annex the Spratlys, it reserves that option for the future. However, given the EEZ claims from neighboring states, this resolution to Spratlys' ownership would probably only generate different disputes over the delimitation of conflicting EEZs.

Should ROC-occupied Itu Aba be determined as the only habitable island in the Spratlys, another EEZ complication arises. Itu Aba's position inside the very western edge of the Philippine EEZ means it would probably have little to no EEZ of its own to its east, but to the west could control the waters in the erstwhile high seas from well north of Northeast Cay to Rifleman Bank.[297] Should these be determined to be internal waters, as Vietnamese or Chinese historic waters, EEZs would be of diminished consequence in any scenario since these would be sovereign seas that would impinge upon the lesser authorities of an EEZ. These historic claims might complicate the South China Sea maritime disputes, however, based upon the extent of Vietnam and China's ambiguous historic claims which probably overlap with the 200-nm EEZ originating from Indonesia's undisputed Natuna Island, between Borneo and Vietnam. Each claim encompasses at least some of the proven Natuna maritime natural gas fields, and thereby embroils Indonesia in the South China Sea dispute.[298] Within any of these scenarios, historic rights, like fishing access to an area or modified delimitation of a zone, may also be pursued against another country's EEZ.[299] In China's view "a claim derived from historic rights may seem more forceful and valid in law than claims simply based upon the EEZ concept," and even if jurisdiction based on historical claims is rejected, they still offer the potential for other historic rights, like access to traditional fishing areas, that cannot be otherwise attained through UNCLOS methods.[300] The combinations of customary and statutory maritime laws with different national interpretations lead to a wide variance in the amount of control that may result, but in most cases occupying islands in the sterile Spratlys will probably gain little in the surrounding waters.[301]

In addition to the delimitation of EEZs, how they are enforced is also very important to the United States. In their implementing domestic laws, both the PRC and ROC claim a 200-nm EEZ and accompanying rights to regulate them under UNCLOS.[302] At well over 400-nm from the nearest Chinese landmass, no Chinese EEZ would influence the Spratly Islands region directly. However, should China start enforcing an EEZ around Itu Aba or other occupied features in the Spratlys, it would challenge foreign military vessels and aircraft to seek permission to operate within these EEZs as it now does in its mainland EEZ.[303] Through its claimed historic rights of special security interests and application of UNCLOS, the PRC requires that activities should "refrain from any threat or use of force" in the EEZ (the intent of UNCLOS definition on transit passage under Part III on straits navigation).[304] China treats its EEZ as a military buffer zone, contending that U.S. military surveillance ships and reconnaissance flights violate the spirit of UNCLOS and China's historic rights in the South China Sea, and seeks to restrict such activities.[305] Thus PRC laws maintain peace in its EEZ by barring foreign military vessels citing Article 58 which directs that states "should comply with the laws and regulations adopted by the coastal State in accordance with the provision of this Convention."[306] If the coastal state's laws are disputed, Chinese scholars declare that deference be given to the

PRC per Article 59, "taking into account the respective importance of the interests involved to the parties as well as to the international community as a whole."[307]

The United States rejects this interpretation contending it is a minority view held by only 27 of the 161 ratifying states (although significantly, Malaysia is also one of the states enforcing a restrictive EEZ).[308] Focusing on one particularly irksome activity, Chinese officials place "military survey and military information gathering . . . into the category of ocean scientific research which requires prior permission from the coastal states."[309] Through applying maritime law in this way, the PRC uses "international law as an adjunct to [its] military forces to achieve anti-access maritime objectives."[310] The triple problem of whether its occupied features can even generate an EEZ, the amount of EEZ such a feature would gain against the neighboring larger landmasses, and whether foreign military vessels or certain activities are barred from an EEZ, make this a very tenuous legal argument for China.[311] However, it could be a useful justification for keeping U.S. vessels out of the South China Sea from a security standpoint, which China could then better defend militarily than legally. In the case of Malaysia, its coastline EEZ does encompass many of the Spratly Islands, but its contention that bars military vessels still keeps it in a minority position within the international community — unless ever evolving international sentiment calls again for a change to the Law of the Sea Treaty.

Continental Shelf Claims.

Although not a jurisdiction that includes a water column like the spaces discussed above, the UNCLOS continental shelf zone is important to adjacent states for the management of nonliving resources and sedentary species on and under the seabed. Extended claims for adjacent ocean floor began with the United States in 1945, and the concept was subsequently incorporated in Article I of the 1958 *Convention on the Continental Shelf* with a limit of 200 meter isobaths or the depth of exploitability.[312] By 1969 the International Court of Justice instituted the "natural prolongation principle," which acknowledged that states had jurisdiction over a much extended continental shelf, although not necessarily from islets or minor coastal features.[313] The resulting UNCLOS articles updating this extended authority were a compromise that allowed a coastal state to control surrounding seabed to the natural length of its continental shelf or to a maximum of 350-nm from the baseline, but also gave geographically challenged states with little adjacent continental shelf at least a 200-nm EEZ that also controlled the seabed below it.[314] Under UNCLOS, states do not need to exploit or occupy the continental shelf to retain exclusive economic rights to its seabed, which includes protrusions from the seabed floor that remain submerged.[315] In Articles 78 and 79, however, it is clear that rights to the continental shelf do not affect the superjacent waters or airspace above it, to include navigation and the unfettered laying of submarine cables and pipelines.[316] The states around the South China Sea supported this greater control over their continental shelf that UNCLOS gave them, and have used it to their economic and political advantage.[317]

These rights over the more distant areas from the claimants' shores come with more obligations than other UNCLOS zones in how they are delimitated. Here the claiming state must first scientifically stake the extent of its continental shelf beyond 200-nm with the UN's Commission on the Limits of the Continental Shelf, which then must qualify it for technical compliance.[318] This is an exacting process that must be completed within 10 years of ratification of UNCLOS, although many developing countries received an extension to May 2009. Even then the Philippines had to rush to meet this closing date in which it also established refined baselines that did not incorporate archipelagic rules, explaining an action cited earlier in this monograph. The Commission cannot qualify an extended continental shelf claim, however, if it is part of a territorial or maritime disagreement with another state, by the Rules of Procedure of the Commission.[319] Consent from the other involved states can be difficult to obtain in the contentious South China Sea environment, as seen in the 2009 joint Vietnamese-Malaysian continental shelf submission to which the PRC and the Philippines objected.[320] Further complicating delimitation of a continental shelf is the potential divergence of an EEZ water column from the continental shelf below it with each assigned to a different jurisdiction.[321] This may occur when the EEZs of a continental state and small island do not overlap, but the natural continental shelf extends out to undercut the island's EEZ, or when negotiated by two parties. Split continental shelf and superjacent EEZ ownership are uncommon, and no resolution in the Spratlys region has resorted to this yet—with the few negotiated settlements instead using a single line for both EEZ and continental shelf.[322] These continental shelf rules, however, make already complicated circumstances around the Spratly Islands that much more difficult to resolve.

South China Sea continental shelf complications are manifested in novel sovereignty claims and over-lapping maritime jurisdictions. China, the Philippines, Malaysia, and Brunei each make territorial claims to submerged features in the Spratlys, rather than mari-time jurisdictional control over them as stipulated in UNCLOS.[323] The three ASEAN states assert sover-eignty over these submerged features based on their extended continental shelf. Unable to resort to historic or archipelagic claims, Malaysia relies on continental shelf extension as its second method to stake sover-eignty over geologic features in addition to discovery and occupation. In its *Continental Shelf Acts* of 1966 and 1969, based on the 1958 *Law of the Sea Treaty*, Malaysia stated its continental shelf is to 200 meters depth or the limit of exploitability. During the UNCLOS for-mulation discussions, Malaysia produced in 1979 its *Map Showing the Territorial Waters and Continental Shelf Boundaries* delimitating its extensive continental shelf and claiming all of its geologic features.[324] Malaysia thus counts sovereignty over 12 islands and reefs:[325]

> based principally on certain continental shelf provi-sions in the 1982 UNCLOS. . . . The clear inference from Malaysia's claims is that a state possessing a con-tinental shelf also possesses sovereign rights over land formations arising seaward from that shelf.[326]

Without an accompanying occupation of Louisa Reef or Rifleman Bank, Brunei's sovereignty claim to both depends solely on its continental shelf and EEZ claims extending to a median line with Viet-nam's claims, as unilaterally made in 1985. Its justi-fication follows arguments similar to those made by

Malaysia.[327] The Philippines claims Kalaya'an through the natural prolongation of its shelf, but also its contiguous nature to the Philippine islands and through occupation of some of the features.[328] For each of these states, UNCLOS is an important way to defend its sovereignty over claimed parts of the Spratly Islands.

As with the other forms of claims, however, those made through UNCLOS have serious weaknesses. The first weakness is legal since, despite these interpretations, much of the international community does not recognize sovereignty claims to territory made through UNCLOS continental shelf articles, a purpose for which they were not intended.[329] The second weakness is geographic. The natural prolongation of a continental shelf stretches only to a point on its slope that plunges to the ocean's depths creating a natural marine boundary. Should a state's shelf plunge close to shore, then it is limited to just its 200-nm EEZ. Malaysia, Brunei, and the Philippines' claims to an extended continental shelf, much less sovereignty over geologic features in the extended area, fall short in the deep Palawan and Manila trenches which effectively moat off the length of the Spratly Islands from the main shores of all three states to their southeast.[330] Thus Malaysia has determined its continental shelf limit only extends as far as its EEZ, while Brunei and the Philippines have not yet declared a continental shelf limit in the South China Sea.[331] The very deep northern South China Sea extends a finger shielding virtually all of the Spratlys from Vietnam's shelf also, to as far south as Rifleman Bank.[332] Thus Vietnam makes no extended continental shelf claims encompassing the Spratlys, but has settled potential overlapping claims with Malaysia through a joint submission to the Commission on the Limits of the Continental Shelf, and has negotiated a boundary line with the PRC in the shallow Gulf of Tonkin.[333] The sub-maritime geographic configuration of the Spratly Islands, then, is that of a relatively shallow sea table isolated by peripheral bands of much deeper waters. Although useful in establishing a jurisdiction over the resources of the contiguous seabed, the extended continental shelf allowed by UNCLOS does not sanction states to claim sovereignty over geologic features, and does not seem to apply geographically to the Spratly Islands even for extended control over its seabed.

The distance and the intervening ocean topography do not allow China to claim a continental shelf extension to the Spratlys from its homeland shores. However, interesting scenarios concerning the EEZ or continental shelf still ensue should China, or another state, convert one of its unique claims in the Spratlys, as already covered, into reality. The most vexing perhaps is the ill-defined Chinese historic claim which could trump other customary and UNCLOS claims in the region. China's historic claim within its South China Sea U-shaped line includes all surface and sub-surface features.[334] This encompassing claim squarely conflicts with EEZ and continental shelf claims made by each of the ASEAN claimant states.[335] In the southwestern part of the South China Sea, the depths are shallow at generally less than 200 meters and a submitted joint extended continental shelf claim splits the region with an equidistance median line between Vietnam and Malaysia.[336] However, China's historic claims cover much of this area and its actions seem to disregard UNCLOS assigned jurisdictions. For instance, in 1992 the PRC created the Crestone oil exploration block around Vanguard and Prince of Wales Banks (the most southwestern of all the Spratly features but also within 200-nm of the Vietnamese baseline, and both banks occupied by Vietnam), in order to conduct drilling operations within what otherwise would be Vietnamese jurisdiction.[337] A similar problem exists in the southern South China Sea, where parts of Malaysia's continental shelf down to only 200 isobaths is claimed by the PRC in its U-shaped line to include North and South Luconia Shoals, Friendship Shoals, and James Shoals. This puts Malaysia's EEZ and continental shelf claim in direct conflict with China's historic claim, although here China has taken no actions to exploit its claim.[338]

Since the Spratly Islands sit on an elevated table of land mostly surrounded by continental shelf ending trenches, should Itu Aba or other islands be judged habitable, each could generate an EEZ and continental shelf extension claim of its own to at least the edge of the Spratlys' shallow sea slope and to where the surrounding states' EEZs or continental shelves did not overlap it.[339] This scenario would remove nearly the entire available high seas to the southwest and north of Itu Aba, to the limits allowed by UNCLOS, from exploitation by other states.[340] In another case, a successful Philippine archipelagic claim to Kalaya'an would gain an EEZ and continental shelf from the new archipelagic baselines that would absorb much of the current high seas areas in the southern South China Sea. The amount of high seas seabed available in the South China Sea is of interest to the United States since high seas areas are exploitable by any state for their resource wealth, and maximizing the availability of deep sea regions and economic return from them is one of the major factors hindering the United States from ratifying UNCLOS. Thus, the extended continental shelf disputes and their resolution will remain a point for the United States to monitor and influence to maintain its own interests and set precedents to its liking.

Territorial and Jurisdiction Claim Summary.

As a "semi-enclosed sea" dominated by overlapping maritime claims, the South China Sea bordering countries are enjoined by UNCLOS Article 123 to "cooperate with each other in the exercise of their rights and performance of their duties" above that normally expected of other maritime states.[341] The shared nature of migratory fish resources, indistinct location of energy sites and advent of lateral drilling, cumulative effect of environmental damage, competing territorial claims and rights, and tight confines that result in confused and conflicting maritime jurisdictions, demonstrate why cooperation is an ideal, if unrealized, goal in the South China Sea.[342] Although a few diplomatic advances to address these myriad regional concerns have been made along the sea's periphery, the states have more often adhered to customary and statuary legal principles that best favor their geopolitical positions.[343] Under this system, the coveted maritime zones of territorial seas, contiguous zones, EEZs, and extended continental shelves depend upon the determination of sovereignty over and classification of claimed land features, which is the core of the Spratly Islands disputes.[344] The by-product of demonstrating effective sovereign control and administration over these claims, unfortunately, has sometimes resulted in aggressive and violent enforcement of national laws, which makes this an important issue to address, in order to prevent miscommunication, accident, or impatience to be used to justify the use of force to settle the disputes.

Until now, however, the disputants have mainly resorted to making outsized claims to maximize any future negotiated outcome, or strengthen their case before arbitration or a tribunal.[345] China, Vietnam, Malaysia, and the Philippines have each asserted sovereignty through discovery and occupation, the most internationally accepted legal method,[346] and, in this, Vietnam leads with 29 garrisons or about as many as the rest of the stations in the Spratlys combined. Vietnam and China also make ill-defined historic claims as another approach to territory, waters, and/or rights, although a method not well-regarded by the international community and, in its collective judgment, lacking sufficient documentation in its application.[347] Under UNCLOS principles, the Philippines has not yet tested its basis for Kalaya'an through the archipelagic articles, while land claims espoused by Malaysia, the Philippines, and Brunei through proximity, EEZs, or continental shelf extensions are dubious for legal or geographic reasons. None of the economically unproductive Spratlys may themselves even generate extended maritime zones, or, if some could, they would probably be given diminished domain against larger land masses under the equitable principle, thereby greatly reducing their significance and the importance of sovereignty over them.[348] Although each of the disputants involved has ratified UNCLOS, each also takes exception to its settlement mechanisms and other select provisions that reduce the overall effectiveness of the treaty to reconcile maritime disputes.[349] Under the current island sovereignty approach in the Spratly Islands dispute, probably "no government today can establish sufficiently substantial legal grounds to validate its claim in the eyes of the international community,"[350] and these legal stances have done little so far to create solutions.[351]

U.S. INTERESTS AND RESPONSES TO THE ISSUES AROUND THE SPRATLY ISLANDS

With this background established, it is clear that events in the South China Sea affect important U.S. interests. The information given so far was presented to better inform policymakers about the involved states' diplomatic, military, police, and legal issues and actions. The issues are complex and contradictory, meaning any U.S. involvement needs to be well informed and nuanced. This section reviews the most relevant U.S. interests in the Spratly Islands region in terms of freedom of navigation, economic activities, and the competing U.S. roles of honest broker for peace and stability among the disputants and regional balancer of power for its security partners. Without maritime jurisdiction or territorial claims of its own in the South China Sea but strong interests in how these issues are resolved, U.S. involvement by necessity is mostly indirect support and grounded in international law, but is also motivated by a political component. Based on these interests, this monograph makes a few recommendations on how the United States may positively influence the situation in the South China Sea to enhance its interests and those of the disputants. Due to the underlying nature of this situation, these recommendations emphasize more the diplomatic, information, and economic elements of U.S. power over military ones.

Although President Barack Obama's administration again made the Asia-Pacific region a top U.S. priority in 2012, this region has been a major U.S. economic and security focus since Commodore Matthew Perry opened Japan in 1854.[352] In particular, five important U.S. global interests are represented there today, including protecting free and unimpeded commerce in the global commons, securing peace and stability among the states, supporting diplomacy and rules-based conduct, ensuring the U.S. military's freedom to operate in compliance with international law, and providing support to U.S. allies and defense partners.[353] Secretary of State Hillary Clinton reiterated these interests specifically for the South China Sea region at the ASEAN Regional Forum in July 2010 emphasizing that:

> The United States, like every nation, has a national interest in freedom of navigation, open access to Asia's maritime commons, and respect for international law in the South China Sea. . . . The United States supports a collaborative diplomatic process by all claimants for resolving the various territorial disputes without coercion. We oppose the use or threat of force by any claimant. While the United States does not take sides on the competing territorial disputes over land features in the South China Sea, we believe claimants should pursue their territorial claims and accompanying rights to maritime space in accordance with the UN Convention on the Law of the Sea. Consistent with customary international law, legitimate claims to maritime space in the South China Sea should be derived solely from legitimate claims to land features.[354]

To achieve these goals, Secretary Clinton emphasized the need to cooperate in areas of common interest in trade, peace, security, and transnational problems like climate change and nuclear proliferation, especially with China.[355] However as an interested party, the United States is also maintaining a relatively balanced playing field which might make it a "little bit easier for the governments in the region to acquire the necessary political will" to resolve their disputes.[356]

Increased U.S. involvement may have started this process in July 2011 when the PRC agreed with Vietnam to implement long-delayed guidelines to govern their disagreements if for no other reason than to limit U.S. involvement.[357] In short, the United States seeks to ensure the legal rights that it and the international community should enjoy in the region, support the legitimate interests of its regional partners, and act upon common ground with China and other involved states to their mutual benefit to improve stability and prosperity in the region.

U.S. Freedom of Navigation Interests.

The issue of immediate concern for the United States, because it may be the most volatile, and the first national interest listed by Secretary Clinton is freedom of navigation.[358] Since UNCLOS was under negotiation in 1979, the U.S. global Freedom of Navigation Program seeks to dispute excessive sea and airspace claims perceived to violate international law by challenging them diplomatically and physically.[359] China, Vietnam, and Malaysia hold restrictive passage views concerning their coastal home waters and potentially in their claimed territorial waters, contiguous zone, and EEZs around the Spratly Islands. These positions place them at odds with most other states' open-use positions, and China sees this issue as an excuse for the United States to continue to intervene in South China Sea issues.[360] The PRC has more aggressively and consistently enforced such restrictions in its claims than any other state — threatening freedom of navigation for all maritime states, and risking armed clashes and instability, especially when backed by its advanced anti-access and area-denial capabilities.[361] After the

1995 PRC occupation of Mischief Reef in the midst of the Philippine EEZ, the United States made clear its stance for freedom of navigation in the region, and in 1998 specifically sent a carrier battle group near the Spratlys to assert American prerogatives.[362] Thus the United States demonstrated how important it considers these rights for itself and those of other interested third parties like Japan.[363]

Despite the chronic tensions, with the growth of prosperity in the region, the need for stability and security, and pursuit of other common interests, the perspective of each party may start to converge in settling their differences. The United States has made progress toward this with Vietnam through a code of conduct concerning activities on the South China Sea, negotiations on navigation, and improved military ties.[364] This better understanding may have contributed to Vietnam relaxing its coastal EEZ transit requirements in 2012 to be more in accord with UNCLOS standards.[365] As the PRC's economy grows and its international commitments expand, China's interests may converge with the more global U.S. views in balancing broad international maritime rights with coastal state rights that China now favors.[366] The PRC is the world's largest exporter and second largest importer, and thus highly depends on the maritime commons to keep its economy growing and has prospered from the open shipping order assured by U.S. naval power. However as China's dependence on seaborne trade continues, it may want to protect its own shipping and sea lines of communication rather than rely on its partner and competitor, the United States, to do so.[367] Among the largest merchant marine fleets and navies in the world, China's perspective should transition to accept the majority interpretation of UNCLOS—meaning more open use of sea jurisdictions and a conventional interpretation of coastal states' rights in its EEZ and territorial sea. Indeed, U.S. interests also seem to be evolving toward embracing stronger coastal states' rights in its own EEZ for economic and environmental protection, thus converging interests may make resolving this issue easier over time to enable completion of some of these suggestions.[368]

To spur this convergence of interests, specific steps should be taken by the United States to defuse the freedom of navigation issue, especially with China where the most active differences lie. The United States could back away from its insistence on exercising its rights to navigation in the South China Sea and its coastal waters in order to ease chronic tensions on this issue. This action was recently recommended by former U.S. National Security Advisor Zbigniew Brzezinski with support of others, but doing this for long could needlessly weaken U.S. and other states' worldwide commitment to UNCLOS open-sea provisions.[369] Instead, as the United States invites the PRC to take a more involved role in ensuring stability and security in the international commons, it should work with China to establish a common understanding on maritime rights in coastal waters and abroad since that is ultimately in both of their interests. The United States and China already have the 1998 *Military Maritime Consultative Agreement* to prevent incidents between them, and although quite imperfectly applied it as a useful confidence building measure.[370] The next step should follow the lead of the 1972 *U.S.-Soviet Union Incidents at Sea Agreement* (INCSEA).[371] This is a successful tool that avoided negative encounters between the two powers, yet complied with international law covering activities like innocent passage through coastal jurisdictions. Through uniform procedures both sides may follow and observe ships from the other side, but may not interfere with their lawful passage, regardless of prior notification, cargo, arms, or type of propulsion.[372] INCSEA is a practical, tested method which could be tailored to reduce tensions, support both sides long-term interests, and accelerate a process of confidence building between the two—especially in the ambiguous Spratly Islands region.[373]

Other forms of cooperation, both military and civilian, could also help build better understanding and trust, and work toward common interests like stability, countercrime, and freedom of navigation in the region as envisioned by Secretary Clinton.[374] A telling example followed the major 2009 incident involving the USS *Impeccable*, after which such incidents ceased as both sides realized that cooperation on issues like North Korea and the global economic recession were more important.[375] While many disputes over issues like Taiwan and military surveillance in the EEZ persist, both sides can build much needed trust and cooperation through existing military and civilian programs like the MMCA, and broaden to new ones to work through their differences. Existing programs to build upon include the "Sino-U.S. Maritime Security Consultation mechanism, the Annual Defense Affairs Consultation mechanism, and the Sino-U.S. Joint Maritime Search and Rescue Exercises," as well as the Container Security Initiative signed in 2003 to combat terrorism.[376] Because of their nature, some new initiatives would be easier to implement such as information exchanges on piracy and terrorism, and maritime disaster mitigation plans. With increased understanding and trust, combined personnel training for humanitarian missions or counterterrorism could follow, with standardized procedures and methods for data and awareness sharing being developed.[377] These could directly improve relations and indirectly support freedom of navigation, and are actions that the U.S. administration and Congress could support with both China and the Southeast Asian states.[378]

The most promising cooperation has been through the U.S. Coast Guard (USCG), which may be more politically acceptable to other governments when emphasizing its enforcement and rescue over its military roles.[379] The various Chinese maritime enforcement agencies and the USCG have already enjoyed cooperative success through the multilateral North Pacific Coast Guard Forum, student training exchanges, detailing Chinese officers aboard USCG cutters in the North Pacific for enforcement actions against Chinese fishermen, and combined bilateral and multilateral exercises in port security, search and rescue, and law enforcement. In 2006, the USCG established permanent liaisons with maritime agencies in four Chinese ministries solidifying a good working relationship with each.[380] The Coast Guard offers other venues of cooperation and confidence building such as sharing its global expertise in protecting port and energy loading operations with Chinese authorities, whose country relies heavily on the safe and secure conduct of maritime energy shipments.[381] Coast Guard cooperation with China is a model to expand into other venues to increase understanding and reduce tensions for issues both sides deem imperative.

Other U.S. military services should also play a role in expanding trust and cooperation between the United States, China, and the Southeast Asian states through greater theater engagement using regionally aligned forces. This is especially true for land forces because armies tend to dominate the region's defense forces in terms of budgets, leadership, and influence. A Department of Defense (DoD)-wide program to assign regionally aligned forces to the region's militaries under U.S. Pacific Command (PACOM) integration would implement security assistance to enhance states' military capabilities. This should allow the states in the dispute to negotiate in a more level environment, build regional understanding with guidance from the Department of State, and build bilateral relations for the United States to act as an honest broker. Regionally aligned forces entail specific units assigned in military-to-military partnerships resulting in a better understanding by U.S. forces of local cultures and languages, geography, military capabilities, and challenges.[382] U.S. units and individuals gain insight and establish enduring personal relations through training-focused visits in platoon to battalion size units.[383] This approach in Southeast Asia especially makes sense since China is the most likely U.S. peer rival, so that recurring engagements with the PRC and its neighbors should build trust, reduce tensions, address differences in fields like maritime access, and establish the United States as a regional conciliator.

The emphasis on land force engagement also makes sense considering that the new AirSea Battle doctrine parcels high-end missions like countering anti-access/area denial to the U.S. Air Force and U.S. Navy in the role of balancing China's power by supporting and protecting the interests of allies and partners in the region. It is left to the land forces and coast guard, playing a smaller part in the defense of the South China Sea region, to support the conciliator role by building trust, capability, and relationships through the U.S. Army, U.S. Marine Corps, and

Special Operations forces as proposed by former Under Secretary of Defense for Policy Michele Flournoy.[384] A more robust regime of exercising, education exchanges, and contingency planning for events of importance to both the United States and the PRC could slowly influence the PLA to better understand American positions, and the United States to understand Chinese positions. As one of the major arbiters over the freedom of navigation dispute within the Chinese system, better relations with the PLA would be helpful in resolving this and other issues both sides face. For U.S. Army forces, upon which the brunt of regional specialization would fall, this alignment concept follows the vision imperative in the Army Chief of Staff's *2012 Army Strategic Planning Guidance,* "Provide modernized and ready, tailored land force capabilities to meet Combatant Commanders' requirements across the range of military operations."[385] The benefits of regionally aligned forces include more effective interactions and support, improved U.S. understanding and interoperability during multinational actions, and better understanding by both sides to allow the United States more access and influence with partners and competitors alike.

Elements of this regionally aligned force proposal exist in the U.S. Army with Special Operations and National Guard units already aligned to the Pacific region, with the Army soon to add active duty conventional forces also. Special Forces units have long specialized to improve partner states' capabilities, build their competence in the world's regions as advisors and operators, and build interoperability and trusted relationships. The 1st Special Forces (SF) Group at Ft Bragg, NC, currently operates under Special Operations Command Pacific covering Southeast Asia, China, and the rest of the Pacific region, along with the U.S. Army National Guard 19th SF Group headquartered in Draper, UT.[386] U.S. Army civil affairs (CA) units also specialize to provide civil-military expertise to conventional forces during theater engagement and full spectrum military operations. The active duty 84th CA Battalion (CAB) at Joint Base Lewis-McCord (JBLM) and 97th CAB at Ft Bragg also align with PACOM, as does the Army Reserve 364th CA Brigade in Portland, OR.[387] As part of its greater regional alignment initiative, in 2014 the Army plans to assign a soon to be designated conventional unit from I Corps, headquartered at JBLM, to support PACOM security cooperation and partnership building activities.[388]

Reserve component forces, when regionally specialized, offer advantages to include greater personnel stability, unique civilian expertise, and some military skills not residing in the active forces, and have thus been particularly effective at achieving high levels of trust, understanding, and cooperation with partners.[389] In PACOM, there are three long-term State Partnership Programs with Southeast Asian states including the Hawaii and Guam Army National Guard partnered with the Armed Forces of the Philippines since 2000, the Hawaii National Guard also partnered with the Indonesian National Armed Forces in 2006,[390] and the People's Army of Vietnam and Oregon National Guard partnered in 2012.[391] State Partnership Programs are sought-after force enablers which are part of PACOM's theater security cooperation plan. These partnerships facilitate stability and security by building partner capacity through exchanging military skills and experience, professional development, exercising, and interagency cooperation.[392]

As U.S. strategy emphasizes the Asia-Pacific region, aligning more Army units to support PACOM's security and engagement plans is a needed initiative for peacetime shaping operations in order to resort less to direct intervention.[393] However, in an era of fiscal austerity, these needed efforts must be adequately sustained and kept efficient to make them viable, be allowed time to take root and grow, and be protected against short-term budget cuts and competing strategic options.[394] One easy-to-correct flaw in the active duty conventional unit regional alignment scheme is that units are only assigned to support a region for 1 year, unlike the long-term engagements of SF, CA, and State Partnership units.[395] Such an arrangement will not build adequate regional expertise, personal relations, or continuity in training and operations to achieve combatant command requirements. Even though active duty unit personnel change more often than reserve component personnel, the institutional links nonetheless remain important and active duty units should be assigned long term regional commitments at the brigade or battalion levels. Another consideration for the Army is that as deployments to Central Command reduce, more units should be regionally aligned to PACOM to allow them to focus on a sub-region like the states bordering the South China Sea.[396] The current scheme has SF, CA, and conventional forces supporting PACOM from Mongolia to New Zealand which dilutes the merits of regionalization. Units assigned to smaller regions or even to critical countries, as done in the State Partnership Program, allow deeper understanding of the region, richer and more frequent contacts with a targeted group of key people, and improved continuity in programs. These alignment efforts would improve U.S. contributions to stability and security in the South China Sea region.

Regional alignment and specialization of units to engagement and shaping tasks does come with problems and challenges. The first challenge is to get the affected states to accept more U.S. involvement, and hence influence, of this type. Although its past ties and an insurgent threat made the Philippines an early and enthusiastic supporter of recent U.S. engagement activities, Vietnam has been a late and reluctant participant because of its need to balance U.S. overtures with those of the Chinese and its past history with the United States. Malaysia, more distant and on better terms with the PRC than the other two, has cordial military contacts with the United States but has not, for instance, elected to partake in the State Partnership Program.[397] As noted earlier in this section, the nature of engagement with the PRC would be different than with the ASEAN countries, emphasizing different tasks and units, as accomplished by the USCG, and must overcome deep historic and geopolitical mistrust.[398]

Regional specialization of U.S. units and personnel is costly and comes at the expense of some combat readiness, since engagement and combat training have limited overlap. The investment in trained personnel and established relationships would have to be protected too, requiring changes in the Army personnel system to retain experienced military members, and minimize out of unit assignments — in essence creating a regimental system in the regionally aligned active forces.[399] Of course, task, equipment, and personnel specialization comes with a price to large unit combat skills, flexibility, and traditional force structure.[400] In a major operation elsewhere that requires the use of PACOM aligned units, all of this specialization will be for naught, and necessary maneuver, fire, and effects skills not as strong as their more often used engagement skills.[401] In austere fiscal times, however, some risk must be assumed in strategy and force structure decisions, as U.S. Army Chief of Staff, General Raymond Odierno, has made clear:

> We always have to be prepared to fight our nation's wars if necessary, but in my mind, it's becoming more and more important that we utilize the Army to be effective in Phase 0, 1 and 2. . . .[402]

To mitigate these risks, the DoD planning considerations of flexibility and reversibility must be inherent qualities in the formation of any regionally aligned specialized units.[403] In austere fiscal times, one potential advantage of regionally aligned forces rotating into a region is that less infrastructure and cost is required in comparison to as many units permanently stationed overseas.[404]

Another very important step for the U.S. Government to better ensure the freedom of navigation rights it now exercises is to formally ratify the UNCLOS treaty. This step is not just to return to equal footing with other members on moral and legal grounds to better support the rules-based-order that the United States espouses, but also to be able to directly guide and protect U.S. interests in international fora and on the seas. The United States signed UNCLOS in 1994 after successfully negotiating an amendment to the document to correct earlier concerns by the industrialized states, but has not formally ratified it through the Senate. The most important provisions of UNCLOS, like maritime jurisdictions and rights of passage, are in accord with U.S. policy so that U.S. domestic laws generally adhere to UNCLOS statutes, as they also do with customary international laws.[405] The Departments of Defense and

State both support ratification to give the United States "greater credibility in invoking the convention's rules and a greater ability to enforce them."[406] This treaty has come before the Senate several times, as recently as 2012, only to be tabled despite bipartisan support, mainly due to economic concerns with Part XI stipulations that cover the deep seabed.[407] A direct American voice in the Law of the Sea Treaty debates would give the United States a stronger voice advocating for freedom of navigation and other U.S. interests, thus countering the historic trend toward circumscribing rights and limiting areas of operation on the high seas. Foreign military navigation rights through an EEZ are a prime example of such restrictions, with 27 countries supporting Chinese, Vietnamese, and Malaysian positions, including major maritime states such as India and Brazil.[408] The Senate needs to ratify this treaty to allow the United States to actively defend its existing maritime legal interests and rights.

Another way to support freedom of navigation rights in the South China Sea is to have China and Vietnam clarify their historic claims. In the modern era of statutory maritime law, sweeping historic claims seem archaic, too incongruous to adjudicate effectively an area as openly used as the South China Sea, and the ensuing disputes unnecessarily hobble economic development and peace.[409] The International Court of Justice has conceded that customary law does not provide for a clear method of adjudicating historic claims, so each case is settled differently based on its specific merits.[410] This gives both Vietnam and China some basis for their historic claims, even while the 1951 International Law Commission criteria make these claims appear weak.[411] Nonetheless, their restrictive interpretations of transit rules in conjunction with expansive Chinese and Vietnamese claims to historic waters, if enforced, could close the very busy South China Sea to military and commercial traffic, which is why the United States and other maritime powers have worked to diminish the doctrine of historic waters and curtail its widespread application.[412] This is in part what Secretary Clinton meant in her earlier quote that "legitimate claims to maritime space in the South China Sea should be derived solely from legitimate claims to land features."[413]

To defuse this problem what is required is that China and Vietnam declare what their historic rights entail—for example, waters, islands, rights to activities, or some combination—and where they are claimed, since China has not explained its U-shaped claim beyond publishing a map.[414] So far, it has cost the historic claimants little to hold these bargaining positions with such sweeping ambiguous claims, and it has become a convenient distraction and delaying tactic. The United States, along with the ASEAN parties and other maritime states, should press China and Vietnam "to particularize or justify its claim" to set the stage for serious negotiations and eventual compromise on specific historic issues.[415] Dropping notorious historic rights claims altogether in favor of current maritime statutory law would simplify the dispute to just occupation doctrine and UNCLOS provisions, although this is an unlikely course, given the multilayered "insurance" approach each state employs. Either method could successfully remove the dead weight of historic claims to allow much needed economic development around the Spratlys, while also reducing the specter of security threats that could derail other initiatives and engulf the region in violence.

Vietnam will find it particularly difficult to uphold its less documented and shorter duration historic claim against China in a legal dispute, nor can it militarily match China's ability to back its historic claim with might (as proven by Vietnam's physical loss of the Paracel Islands, also a Vietnamese historic claim, to Chinese occupation). However, Vietnam does have a strong occupation presence in the Spratlys upon which to rely. It might be convinced to transform its undefined historic claims for the steadier position of occupation and UNCLOS laws, especially if given strong international support for current Vietnamese island sovereignty, and coastal EEZ and continental shelf claims that comply with UNCLOS. Such a policy should garner consistent U.S. support in accordance with Secretary Clinton's call for settling legitimate territorial and maritime claims using UNCLOS and accepted international customary law. Indeed, UNCLOS provisions for the EEZ and continental shelf were meant in part to replace historic claims, and Vietnam might be a good candidate to do this.[416] To improve the deal, the international community should also support specific historic economic rights for Vietnam for well-documented activities like fishing, which would include assured access to the area but not jurisdiction over it.[417] In return for internationally recognized claims and rights, Vietnam would agree to fully abide by majority interpretations of UNCLOS to include freedom of navigation in its EEZ and innocent passage in its territorial seas, and drop its claim to historic waters or title in the South China Sea.

Unfortunately, there may be less incentive for China to clarify any of its claims in the Spratly Islands. There are legal and political advantages for China to obscure its historic, other customary, and UNCLOS based claims by "rigidly refus[ing] to clarify the basis for its claims."[418] China's historic claims are challenged in the international community. Its occupation claims (except for Taiwan's Itu Aba) are also on literal and figurative shifting ground, and it has little recourse to coastal EEZ or proximity claims in the Spratly Islands. An ambiguous stance therefore allows China to shift its claim-support as circumstances dictate and not be held accountable to defend its claims in the context of international law, "even as the growth of its military and maritime assets gain physical leverage over its weaker neighbors."[419] China may use ambiguity as a way to deflect U.S. and other outside maritime states' involvement by obscuring issues during negotiations, and thereby keep what it considers regional bilateral issues from being internationalized.[420] The lack of specificity may also result from political divides on these issues within the government of the PRC, which may make any change in policy arduous.[421] China may be playing a weak hand by keeping it close to its chest.

However, there may be influential elements in the Chinese government that see its international role growing and that its current restrictive naviga-tion policy not only sets the PRC at odds with most other states, but also with its own future needs as an emerging world power desiring access to littoral re-gions around the world. Among its divergent agen-cies, the argument might prevail that the PRC should rely on its growing navy for defense of its home wa-ters rather than weaker legalistic methods which may later be used against it, especially if mutually accept-able methods to open EEZs to navigation are made in arrangements similar to INCSEA. At least one com-mentator has noted that the PRC's recent legislation and policy statements seem to be part of a trend of historic waters being "gradually turned into the EEZ and continental shelf of the Paracel and Spratly archipelagos," without actually foregoing yet its assertions for historic rights.[422] Most parties would not want the United States to be directly involved in negotiating any such schemes, but it could, nonetheless, support such solutions indirectly through its good offices, expertise, and material support.

U.S. Economic Interests.

Open economic access to the South China Sea maritime commons is the second U.S. interest listed by Secretary Clinton.[423] PACOM's regional strategy also acknowledges the importance of open access to the shared commons in the Asia-Pacific region, adding "that continued economic prosperity is tied to the peaceful rise of China as an economic and military power,"[424] making this economic issue one also linked to security. Within the bounds of UNCLOS, economic access includes universal rights for commercial shipping and the opportunity to exploit the natural resources of the high seas. Short of open conflict or blockade, however, the only threat to commercial passage in the South China Sea is its designation as historic waters which would subject passage to restrictions similar to transiting internal waters, worse than what foreign military craft have faced in PRC and Vietnamese EEZs. To date this remains just a possibility since neither China nor Vietnam try to regulate commercial traffic through their claimed historic waters or maritime jurisdictions.[425] Thus, the issue of commercial passage through the South China Sea, an important U.S. national interest, is directly linked to the determination of historic waters in the region.

If commercial navigation is not currently a problem, commercial exploitation of South China Sea resources may be. By the UNCLOS preamble, the high seas are interpreted as:

> the area of the seabed and ocean floor and the subsoil thereof, beyond the limits of national jurisdiction, as well as its resources, are the common heritage of mankind, the exploration and exploitation of which shall be carried out for the benefit of mankind."[426]

Although UNCLOS does regulate fishing and mineral extraction that are the most common forms of economic use in these deep sea areas,[427] developed countries with high-end technology, expertise, and capital have an advantage in exploiting "the common heritage of mankind." For this reason, UNCLOS includes a regime through the International Sea-Bed Authority (ISA) to regulate the remote gathering of strategic metals from the seabed floor, considered the potentially most lucrative activity of the high seas, and to provide for distribution of part of the gained profits to all nations.[428] As a semi-enclosed sea, however, Article 123 also gives the bordering states rights and duties to manage, conserve, and exploit the living resources of the sea and protect the marine environment,[429] which raises questions about who will manage which parts of these high seas. None of the South China Sea parties, especially China, are likely to accept opening their sea's bounty to shared profits under ISA rules.[430] Each of the South China Sea states has demonstrated its desire to maximize natural resource gains from the sea, which this monograph has shown is a major factor in the disputes and violence among them.[431] U.S. interests in the economic uses of the high seas would be governed by UNCLOS if the United States joins, but potentially also by the South China Sea neighbors based on their maritime claims or cooperative administration as a semi-enclosed sea.[432]

Disregarding the historic waters issue, which would make exploitation of this sea by other states moot, the tangled claims in the South China Sea leave in doubt how much may be high sea, and how much are within national jurisdictions. If measured as just EEZs from coastal baselines without any islands generating more than territorial waters — the position taken by Vietnam, Malaysia, and the Philippines — then high seas would be the elongated center of the South China Sea from north of Macclesfield Bank, down to and including the western Spratly Islands to southwest of Rifleman Bank.[433] Should China succeed in its claim for the Paracel Islands and prove they are habitable, which is better supported than any of the Spratlys being so designated, a large swath around Macclesfield Bank would become Chinese EEZ and significantly reduce the size of the northern high seas area.[434] Should Itu Aba or other Spratly Islands be awarded to a state and recognized as habitable, or if the Philippines establishes its claim to Kalaya'an through archipelagic rules, then nearly all of the South China Sea would be blotted from high sea status because the newly established EEZs would butt up against those from the main lands.[435] Commercial rights to sea life, mineral, and energy resources on the high seas depends in part on how territorial claims and maritime jurisdictions are delimitated based on island sovereignty, because the remainder becomes high seas for any state's access. How this is resolved is of interest to the United States to ensure open access to the high seas here and elsewhere in the world, and to maintain the peace.

U.S. economic interests face two problems then in the Spratly Islands region: the UNCLOS rules concerning exploitation of the high seas, and whether there may even be high seas available in the area. The United States has not formally ratified UNCLOS for several reasons, a main one is that objections to Part XI cover exploitation of the deep seabed. Its provisions are considered statist and not free-market oriented, and the ISA is expensive and inefficient.[436] Opponents also see little gain in the South China Sea for U.S. ratification since the overlapping disputes would not only remain but have no compulsory settlement agreement, and maritime jurisdiction issues like freedom of navigation are exempt from mandatory arbitration mechanisms. Thus, they argue, these political issues do no change whether the United States is a member or not.[437] The irony of opposing U.S. entry to UNCLOS is that in the nearly 30 years since it was written, no country or corporation, including the United States, has been successful in commercially mining for high seas mineral resources, but the United States, which has the world's largest aggregate EEZ, benefits from the economic and environmental protection of its littoral that UNCLOS provides.[438] By its present stance, the United States gains freedom from the ISA to potentially mine sea bed resources some day since it does not need to be a member of UNCLOS to exploit international waters under customary law, but it loses the advantages of being inside the Sea Treaty system to guide it and employ its provisions for future U.S. benefit.

Of greater importance for U.S. interests than the rules covering the economic exploitation of the high seas are the regimes that may govern these waters. In addition to the different possibilities for maritime jurisdictions based on awarded sovereignty presented herein, several multilateral governing regimes have been proposed, especially diplomatic solutions relying on joint development of the sovereign and/or international zones of the South China Sea. Indonesian scholar Hasjim Djalal proposed a "doughnut formula" in which the international waters at the center of the South China Sea would be managed by the neighboring states as a Joint Development Zone (JDZ) to share resources, or a less robust Joint Management Zone (JMZ) to facilitate research and measures to protect the environment and fishing stocks per UNCLOS Article 123.[439] In these arrangements, jurisdiction claims are retained by states in disputed areas, but each state has a part in the exploration, development, or protection based on a sharing agreement in ways that could also become confidence building measures.[440] On a small scale, successful joint development areas already operate between Vietnam and Malaysia (with weak joint commission oversight), and Thailand and Malaysia (with strong oversight).[441] Such cooperative agreements could be expanded to be multilateral and cover some or all of the Spratly Islands or the entire South China Sea. By sharing resources and finally generating some of its economic potential, joint management could calm the conflicts among the South China Sea parties.

Several models of joint development have been offered, which vary in how much sovereignty the group claims over the high seas, how dominant anyone state is in controlling the region's administration, and the acceptance of such solutions and participation by the international community. One precedent proposed is to apply the Svalbard Treaty of 1920 as a model for the Spratly Islands, granting one state restricted powers as the administrator over the islands, while other treaty participants would retain wide economic rights to the area and continue to use currently occupied land features which would be demilitarized.[442] Which country would be given control would be contentious with China vying as the dominant power (militarily, in its historic assertion, and as occupier of Itu Aba the key Spratly land feature) to which the others would probably not agree. Valencia, Van Dyke, and Ludwig refine this concept, adding a Spratly Management Authority administered in one of three ways: shares are given and China holds a plurality stake; the area is managed through bilateral agreements between China and the other states; or the Authority is open to admittance by all states that ratify a Svalbard-like "Spratly Islands Treaty."[443] This third solution awards sovereignty of the islands to a state, but shares its development and profits with other states that invest under the agreement. Opening the treaty to all states to sign and participate would give it wider international legitimacy that the current unilateral state claims lack, and could ensure that the high seas remain international for economic development.

A variation to this Svalbard solution is that the disputant states submit to UNCLOS archipelagic rules in defining the Spratlys and then divide interests in the entity. In this case, one of the weakest states, the Philippines, would have to be the sovereign as the only eligible archipelagic state. The responsibilities and benefits for the economic development and administration of the region could be split among the five claimants in several ways, but if coastline length on the South China Sea were used (which is what the International Court of Justice uses when adjusting for fairness under the "equity principle"), the shares would be: PRC and Taiwan, 37 percent; the Philippines, 28 percent; Vietnam, 20 percent; Malaysia 14, percent; and Brunei, 2 percent.[444] This solution, too, would award clear sovereignty to one state, and, as part of an archipelago, the Spratlys would have baselines that generate an EEZ which would encompass most of the current high seas. This solution fulfills Secretary Clinton's goals of land and maritime claims based on recognized international (UNCLOS) law in a collaborative diplomatic process.[445] Awarding sovereignty to one of the militarily and economically weakest states in the region might hold appeal to the other disputants, especially if China gets the most shares. The United States might also concur with a traditional ally as the choice. This solution would eliminate, however, most of the high seas areas in the South China Sea, and shut out other states from use of the region.

The opposite approach to assigning sovereignty over the islands and sharing in their economic development is to follow the Antarctica Treaty System model in the Spratlys. Applying Antarctic Treaty principles here would envisage that all land claims and resource interests be set aside (neither recognized nor renounced), the region be demilitarized, and environmental protections and scientific research take precedence.[446] Rather than a state, an international body like the proposed "International Spratly Authority" composed of treaty members with demonstrated interests in the region, would oversee the area's economic development under a scheme similar to the Convention on the Regulation of Antarctic Mineral Resource Activities. The region could also become a marine park under rules similar to Antarctica's Environmental Protection Protocol and UNCLOS provisions enjoining states around a semi-enclosed sea to protect its environment.[447] The languishing Coordinating Body of the Seas of East Asia (COBSEA) could be revitalized under this scheme to better coordinate and manage fisheries and protection of the environment.[448] Under this scheme, no sovereignty is awarded, and the waters remain international. Occupying states could retain their bases, as research stations are maintained in Antarctica, but would have to be demilitarized. Although China, Malaysia, Japan, and the United States are among the signatories of the Antarctic Treaty, a similar South China Sea Treaty would probably be rejected by the claiming states, especially the dominant state China, for their loss of economic opportunity and reduced security interests. For the United States, this solution meets its stated national interests and uses a collective diplomatic process to arrive at a solution. But without the support of the South China Sea states, there is little prospect for long-term security or stability; thus, this would not be a viable option.

The economic concern for the United States in these schemes is whether such development in the high seas is a venture under UNCLOS or customary law provisions that recognize all states' rights, or whether the high seas are to be controlled and administered by a group entity. In some of these options, a jointly shared regional commons is formed around the Spratlys through combining historic interests or the convenient interpretation that maritime jurisdictions are generated from the islands. The resulting commons then pools the region's resources for mutual benefit of the claimants. This type of approach is not explicitly sanctioned in UNCLOS, but has international legal precedent in which Honduras, Nicaragua, and El Salvador were given "condominium" ownership in the Gulf of Fonseca case. A similar combination of nation-

93

al maritime jurisdictions and shared claims through a condominium would eliminate all international waters from the South China Sea.[449] Although still very hypothetical, such joint solutions, that liberally interpret international law to economically benefit regional states and bring peace and security to the region at the expense of the economic interests of outside parties, pose a dilemma for the United States. A condominium solution may impede the potential to exploit the high seas in the region, or introduce undetermined restrictions to navigation, both contrary to U.S. interests. On the other hand, such a solution would promote peace and stability among the states through diplomatic processes, and support economic development and expand energy availability in a region where it is sorely needed. The ensuing conflict in U.S. goals for the region means that, if such solutions are seriously proposed, they need to include wide international influence to balance all interests and be open to all states much like the Svalbard Treaty. Although these would be difficult negotiations, if successful, they would produce enduring and positive results for all of the parties involved.

Some of these joint development solutions would follow PRC communist party leader Deng Xiaoping's proclamation in the early 1990s that in the South China Sea, "sovereignty is ours, set aside disputes, pursue joint development," a policy which subsequent Chinese leaders have embraced, but of which other leaders are wary.[450] This enduring Chinese perspective has burdened cooperative proposals and the DOC, signed in 2002 by the PRC and ASEAN, which established a political framework for peace and stability in the region, and potential for cooperative development agreements among the parties.[451] The only multilateral economic arrangement pursued so far has been the JMSU in 2005 in which the state oil companies from the PRC, Vietnam, and the Philippines agreed to conduct joint seismic surveys for oil in their disputed areas as a confidence building measure.[452] The agreement expired in acrimony in 2008, however, because the smaller states believed the PRC only wished to explore in disputed areas near their shores, but not in contested areas in which China was unilaterally exploiting.[453] Despite this failure and China's overbearing policy, U.S. policy supports joint projects in the region such as the start of drafting a code of conduct to the DOC in 2011.[454] The United States also supports Philippine President Benigno Aquino's proposal for the multilateral Zone of Peace, Freedom, Friendship, and Cooperation to establish joint research and economic development bodies over undisputed areas, which has proven difficult to implement since everything in the region seems disputed.[455]

Any joint development or governing deal in the South China Sea is burdened by the lack of compromise and division among the ASEAN countries, and distrust of a domineering PRC as demonstrated in this monograph.[456] The PRC, for its part, is also suspicious that other states are encroaching on its claims and prosperity.[457] An analysis of this situation by the International Crisis Group warns that:

> Joint development, while an opportunity for claimants to cooperate and thereby reduce tensions, has stalled as claimants resist China's demands that they first accept its sovereignty over disputed areas. The failure to reduce the risks of conflict, combined with the internal economic and political factors . . . are pushing claimants toward more assertive behavior. . . . [C]laimants would benefit from taking concrete steps toward the

joint management of hydrocarbon and fishing resources, as well as toward reaching a common ground
on the development of a mechanism to mitigate or
de-escalate incidents, even if they cannot agree on an
overall approach to dispute resolution.[458]

Thus, it is unlikely that China will enter into
negotiations or a cooperative economic agreement as
an equal with other regional sovereign states, which
affects the United States and ASEAN countries'
approaches in this region.[459] The proposals discussed
here show that the South China Sea disputes persist
not for lack of innovative solutions, but because of
the lack of political will and domestic agendas of the
participants.

United States: Honest Broker or Balancer?

Based on U.S. interests and policies presented so
far, how should the United States engage in the South
China Sea disputes? It can play one of two roles, and
over time will probably engage in both as it pursues
its interests in navigation and economic development,
and as changing circumstances dictate. The first role
is that of honest broker among the disputants help-
ing, along with other states, to resolve these thorny
issues through "respect for international law . . . collaborative diplomatic process . . . without coercion
. . . [and] not take sides. . ." as proposed by Secretary Clinton.[460] The new Secretary of Defense, Chuck
Hagel, has also stressed addressing threats through
engagement.[461] The other role is that of balancer
recognizing that the sovereign states in the region
do not meet on a level playing field, and that U.S.
commitments and national interests obligate the Unit-

ed States to take some parochial positions for its own benefit or to support an enduring overall solution.[462] These U.S. approaches compensate for the PRC strategy in which claims for land sovereignty and maritime delimitation are conducted bilaterally to gain advantage over weaker claimants, while lesser and more encompassing issues like safety, anti-crime, and environmental protection may follow a multilateral approach.[463] Brzezinski recently summed up this dual role for the United States as the "balancer and conciliator between the major powers in the East."[464] This could be similar to the U.S. position between Taiwan and the PRC in that it both supports and restrains its partner while also constructively engaging a sometime competitor and collaborator. For this reason, harmonizing these two roles is crucial to American, ASEAN, and Chinese long-term interests in regional peace, cooperation, and prosperity.

When it serves to advance solutions in the Spratly Islands, the United States should play the role of honest broker because it shares common goals and interests for peace and stability with China and the ASEAN states.[465] Since its recent rise to regional power, China and the United States keep returning to a "constructive strategic partnership," despite intermittent intervening crises, because their long-term interests ultimately overlap and the need to manage them together continues.[466] The role of honest broker in the South China Sea will encourage this engagement with China as equals, while offering additional benefits of allowing the United States to represent general international interests in the region, and dampen ASEAN claimants' potential to overplay a position when the United States acts as a balancer on their behalf.[467] As an honest broker, U.S. policy in National Security Presidential Directive (NSPD) 41 seeks to:

enhanc[e] international relationships and promot[e] the integration of U.S. allies and international and private sector partners into an improved global maritime security framework to advance common security interests in the Maritime Domain.[468]

Following this line, PACOM's strategy supports multilateral approaches with regional groups like ASEAN to develop relationships that build trust and reinforce international norms, and also engages with China to achieve a variety of common bilateral and multilateral goals.[469] Secretary Clinton especially singled out the long awaited full code of conduct negotiations, that will supplement the 2002 DOC, in which the United States as a conciliator is "prepared to facilitate initiatives and confidence building measures" among the parties.[470] Such measures build the necessary trust in the United States to help respond to crises or when support is needed, and is simply good diplomatic practice in a tense region with important U.S. interests.[471]

U.S. and regional state interests are best served with an involved United States that can play the conciliator role when needed. This monograph has outlined why U.S. interests are served this way, but so are regional stability and peace. Without American involvement stronger states may assert themselves in the disputes more, while, through miscalculation or domestic pressure, weaker states may start incidents they may not be able to contain.[472] Among the regional powers, neither China nor ASEAN, with substantial direct interests in the dispute, nor Japan, with indirect interests similar to the United States but with a negative legacy that makes it distrusted in the region, can substitute in this role.[473] Indonesia, through the Track II talks it has hosted since 1990, has played the role of diplomatic conciliator in the South China Sea disputes, but Indonesia, too, has maritime conflicts with China and lacks the substantial resources that the United States can bring to influencing solutions.[474] The United States can be a good mediator because it has enough interests in the disputes to remain engaged, the power to be heeded in council, important overlapping interests with each party (especially China) to be cautious and balanced, sufficient distance from the region to prefer local initiatives and solutions, and is willing to include all affected states in the process through programs like its Global Maritime Partnership.[475] This U.S. stance has been called "active neutrality," but when necessary that includes direct actions like confronting the PRC when U.S. navigation interests are threatened, while also restraining an ally, such as when President Obama reminded President Aquino, when looking for more support for Philippine claims, that, "The United States will provide support for principled negotiations and a peaceful resolution, but not specific outcomes."[476] The United States is thus an important factor in promoting the peaceful and prosperous environment to which China and the other Asian states have contributed and mutually benefited, but the United States has done so by allowing the states involved to take the initiative for mediation.[477]

As shown, however, the U.S. position has not been strictly neutral, and the United States has become involved in disputes when deemed necessary. Until the 1995 Mischief Reef incident, the United States did not intervene in the Spratlys because the disputes did not affect global stability or major U.S. interests. Since the end of the Cold War, as the United States has perceived increasing threats to the sea lanes and potential for military conflict in the South China Sea, Chinese observers believe that U.S. policy has evolved from active neutrality to "active concern," and as a result has become more willing to intervene.[478] PRC officials see a less impartial United States siding with the Southeast Asian states at its expense, at least indirectly if not in public, and that the United States may be slowly abandoning neutrality.[479] The strategic shift of focus to the Pacific Rim and East Asia is a major example of a more active and potentially parochial role for the United States. The ASEAN states have found China's claims and behavior in the region to be overbearing and threatening, and quietly welcome the U.S. commitment to deterring potential aggression from the PRC to ensure security and allow negotiations toward a settlement.[480] Their fear is that when vital Chinese interests have been threatened, the PRC has resorted to conflict to protect them, even against a superior power, [481] and there is a possibility that the South China Sea may prove to be one of those core Chinese interests.[482] Through its military, economic, and political power; cultivated ties with the disputants; and its own national interests; the United States alone may be the "external balancer providing security guarantees to whatever state may be attacked by another, and thereby making regional balances-of-power much less significant."[483]

Partiality in the disputes is due in part because the United States holds formal defense treaty alliances with Japan and the Philippines. The United States and the Philippines share a 1951 Mutual Defense Treaty which was reaffirmed by both defense chiefs in June 2013. It is usually interpreted not to include defending the disputed Spratly Islands, however, and the United States did not, for instance, intervene in the Philippine's Mischief Reef incident with the PRC.[484] However, the treaty also allows the Philippines to request assistance from the United States if any of its forces are attacked anywhere in the Pacific region, which could apply to some scenarios in the South China Sea. The Southeast Asia Collective Defense Treaty also requires the United States to take action for the common defense (both the Philippines and Thailand) if peace in the treaty area is threatened; the treaty area specifically includes the South China Sea.[485] Although the organization part of the Southeast Asia Treaty Organization (SEATO) dissolved in 1977, the collective defense treaty and its obligations remain in effect.[486] The Obama administration has also worked to promote more unity within ASEAN, which has no real defense arrangement, to better withstand Chinese pressure. To this end PACOM's strategy seeks to strengthen relationships with ASEAN and its states, and specifically "enhance our partnerships with Indonesia, Malaysia, Singapore, Vietnam, and others to advance common interests and address shared threats."[487] Brzezinski concludes that in Asia the United States should play the dual role of conciliator and regional balancer, as the United Kingdom (UK) did in 19th-century European politics, by "mediating conflicts and offsetting power imbalances among potential rivals."[488]

American balancing actions have weighed against China when needed but usually in a way to not endanger its role as conciliator. In 2010, the United States maneuvered the ARF agenda to make the South China Sea disputes a primary topic for multilateral, not bilateral, discussions; and at the subsequent ARF meeting in Hanoi Secretary Clinton denounced unilateral actions in the South China Sea and supported the need for all parties to negotiate a code of conduct. This indirectly condemned China for both its aggressive actions and its recalcitrance to an already agreed to procedure, while offering the olive branch of conciliation at the same time to rectify the situation.[489] Balancing also means strengthening the ASEAN states' military capabilities through establishing or strengthening military cooperation agreements and forward deploying U.S. forces into East Asia.[490] These moves support U.S. interests in the South China Sea as declared by Secretary Clinton, thereby "internationalizing" the disputes to the consternation of the PRC which loses diplomatic and military clout.[491] U.S. intervention has been overt as well. The United States, for instance, loudly condemned Chinese actions to establish the Sansha municipality on the South China Sea islands, while not criticizing similar earlier actions by Vietnam and the Philippines.[492] U.S. officials have also described Chinese jurisdiction claims within the U-shaped line as excessive, and thereby some analysts believe "the United States is now a disputant in the South China Sea disputes."[493] However, for the United States such measures provide the region the military security needed for diplomacy to operate on a relatively level field, or as a past Vietnamese ambassador bluntly stated, "If the United States does not show some signs of support for the smaller countries on this issue, Vietnam will have no choice but to accommodate China. . . ."[494]

The United States must adroitly manage its dual roles. Because of its own interests and formal obligations, the United States should continue to play the balancer role, but needs to account for the significant benefits and hazards to the region in terms of peace and stability.[495] U.S. involvement acts to deter the use of force, balancing weaker regional states' power with that of the PRC, and thereby constraining the parties to work within a diplomatic and legal framework (while also drawing the smaller states closer to the United States).[496] For instance, after Secretary Clinton's greater interest in the South China Seas at the 2010 ARF, a Vietnamese diplomat could exclaim that China did not take Vietnam seriously before, but "they talk to us now."[497] The United States must be alert, however, to not let such support embolden some states and increase regional instability, as a Philippine presidential spokesperson appeared to do when commenting that the U.S. presence "bolsters our ability to assert our sovereignty over certain areas."[498] United States support to a common ASEAN position in the South China Seas could be seen as hostile by the Chinese and make the region more violent.[499] Chinese observers believe that its bilateral engagements with the other states were beneficial to the region until U.S. provocations internationalized the disputes through "gunboat" policy.[500] Too much or misapplied U.S. support in the region will not only alienate China, but could also sow discord among the ASEAN states, which runs counter to American intentions for ASEAN unity to balance Chinese power.[501]

Because of many mutual interests and strong economic embrace, the United States must remain delicate and agile in its involvement in the region, but it must remain involved because there is no viable alternative state for the roles it plays. As an honest broker to the region, it offers resources and a proclivity for mediation that in the long run will result in solutions yielding a more stable, prosperous, and peaceful region based on the disputants' participation. As a balancer, the United States sets the conditions needed for all states to engage as bilateral or multilateral equals in the spirit of international law. Because the United States does this to further its own interests in conjunction with those of China and the ASEAN states, its commitment to these goals should be significant and enduring through building trust and reinforcing international norms. The United States alone can deter aggression by any state or combination of states, and is sometimes obligated by treaty to do so. China and the ASEAN states should accept the United States as an honest broker to keep America's role relatively neutral, but also allow it to balance to ensure better solutions are determined in equal negotiations or under international law. Should the United States play its dual roles correctly, it can be called upon to be both mediator and deterrent to aggression as envisioned by former Philippine President Fidel Ramos.[502] Should the United States over emphasize either role, it could embolden aggression by appearing too weak to enforce stability or too partisan to contribute to peace. Thus, Brzezinski concludes, "If the United States and China can accommodate each other on a broad range of issues, the prospects for stability in Asia will be greatly increased."[503]

CONCLUSION

The region around the Spratly Islands and the South China Sea may be called the Dangerous Ground indeed. It is fraught with physical, economic, political, and military hazards that require delicate navigation. This region is important to the economies of the surrounding states in terms of the fish they eat and sell and the vast potential for natural gas and oil needed to fuel their growing economies. This bonanza of riches spurs much of the out-sized claims in the region that result in diplomatic and physical clashes. This is unfortunate because the conditions these confrontations create reduce outside investment in the region, squander resources through their unregulated use, and hinder the states from cooperating for their mutual economic benefit. The high flow of maritime commerce through the South China Sea is also crucial to the economic well-being of the region and the world. Although the waters around the Spratly Islands are economically important, the islands themselves have not been. However, occupation of the islands dictate control of the surrounding sea's wealth and navigation, and could legally or militarily control maritime traffic and the waters' economic exploitation. Thus, the land features are important to these states for security purposes, and because possession of them may be the key to controlling the coveted surrounding waters. Claim and authority over these land features is strengthened by the establishment of around 50 remote military garrisons on these islets, which increases the militarization of the dispute with an increased risk of conflict.

Although direct military confrontations among the claimant states have diminished since the 1990s, civilian enforcement agencies have been active in protecting claimed spaces sometimes employing violence resulting in deaths. Because partner countries rely on the United States to ensure stability in the South China Sea and to address its own interests in maintaining freedom of navigation rights and economic development of the international sea bed, the United States should remain engaged with the South China Sea states on issues of mutual concern. The United States has also been embroiled in the region through confrontation with the PRC over rights of navigation through claimed waters and in support of partners and allies. The United States must be wary, then, of both overplaying its position or having an ally do so and alienating the PRC, or allowing the PRC to use the South China Sea as a crucible in which to test American resolve or bait a trap as part of a confrontational military rise. To better address these concerns, policymakers need to understand the underlying problems and conflicting claims that threaten security and prosperity in this region.

The use of customary and UNCLOS law in establishing claims to the Spratlys and surrounding waters helps explain both the perspectives of the disputants and how they have in part interacted with each other and the United States on the issues of rights and claims. Their legal positions are especially important for American policymakers as they inform possible solutions and suggest how to contribute to peace and prosperity in the region. Three key legal questions must be answered to help sort the disputes: sovereignty over the islets, the nature of a claimed land feature, and the delimitation of maritime jurisdiction. Sovereignty is claimed through customary law, with China and Vietnam both using historic doctrine to claim the entire South China Sea, while they also use the doctrine of occupation to claim some land features, the method which the Philippines and Malaysia also employ. The establishment of UNCLOS precepts made otherwise unproductive land features valuable. Establishing control over them using customary law has sometimes spurred clashes.

Since the historic claims are expansive and unconvincingly documented in the views of many experts, claims made through discovery and occupation are more influential. In this, Vietnam, the Philippines, Malaysia, the PRC, and Taiwan each lay claim to parts of Spratly features based on their status as once *res nullis* during various times in modern history. Taiwan also claims all of the land features based on its occupation of the largest island which is an interpretation of customary law that is in dispute. The Philippines Kalaya'an claim to most of the islands through its proximity is not backed with effective occupation. Each of these states supports its claims with efforts at effective administration through establishing laws governing its possessions under municipal governments, economic activities, or military occupation. Each state's claims are also disputed with counter-claims by other South China Sea states leaving physical possession of a feature the surest guide to ownership with no state holding effective legal sovereignty over all. General recognition of the current occupation situation of the Spratly Islands would settle some of the disputes, but could launch other dangerous problems through a new round of seizures, claims, and possible violence to gain the potential benefits of as yet unoccupied land features.

Developed to reflect modern interpretations of international law, UNCLOS offers guidance to maritime disputes in the South China Sea but is not a comprehensive solution. Once sovereignty of a land feature is determined, UNCLOS stipulates its jurisdiction over surrounding waters based on its human characteristics. This process is meant to maintain tranquility in the ocean commons through establishing various maritime zones with graduated degrees of sovereign rights for the state. Islands designated as inhabitable or economically viable accrue more consideration than uninhabitable rocks and other features, making only some of the occupied areas in the Spratlys eligible to establish a modest maritime jurisdiction, and probably none meet the habitable standard to garner full jurisdiction. This would leave the waters around the Spratlys mainly under the maritime control of the surrounding land masses, or as international waters unless the claiming states cooperate under the guise of the enclosed sea rules to establish a joint maritime zone.

Once sovereignty and feature type are determined, zones of authority may be established by the occupying state depending on the distance from its established shore baseline. Internal, archipelagic, and historic waters are maritime variations of near-full sovereign control, which could be disruptive to economic and navigation activities if awarded to any state to govern all of the Spratly waters. Vietnam or China, for instance, could control the entire South China Sea if either historic claim was affirmed, or the Philippines would control its Kalaya'an claim with an extensive EEZ if the Spratlys were determined to be an extension of the Philippine archipelago. Islands above the high tide mark establish territorial waters and a contiguous zone, which would carve 24-nm zones like Swiss cheese around the Spratlys, but should allow innocent passage even if restricting most other maritime activities. However, Vietnam, Malaysia, and China do not recognize innocent passage for naval ships, which makes such zones a major concern for the U.S. Government.

Since the length of the 200-nm EEZ allows much potential overlap among land masses and islands in the semi-enclosed South China Sea, their delimitation through equidistant or equitable principles affects jurisdiction, and, like territorial waters, some states restrict military activities within the EEZ beyond the economic regulation normally allowed. Habitability of an island is a significant issue for EEZ delimitation since only populated or economically viable islands may claim an EEZ. The awarding of an EEZ under several scenarios then affects freedom of navigation and the potential for U.S. economic development in otherwise international waters. Although such arguments by claimants for more restrictions in these zones are tenuous, they could be useful justification to cover military actions by states like China, which is the most active in enforcing a restrictive EEZ.

Freedom of navigation in the South China Sea is the most immediate concern for the United States to ensure naval vessels retain all the rights of access allowed in the region under international maritime law. Current policies in China, Vietnam, and Malaysia restrict foreign naval activity in their zones beyond that normally attributed to UNCLOS. This is a bad precedent for U.S. maritime access around the world, but the United States has options to improve the situation in the South China Sea. First, it has already signed the MMCA with the PRC to reduce the number of maritime incidents between the two countries. Concluding an *Incidents at Sea Agreement* with the PRC would clarify further the rights and responsibilities between the two, especially when operating within each other's maritime jurisdictions while also remaining fully compliant with international law and significantly reducing the potential for future clashes. Other forms of government to government interaction would build confidence in present and future agreements, leverage common interests, as the USCG has done so well with its PRC counterparts, and would also reduce tensions in the region to enhance freedom of navigation.

Through engagement activities of regionally aligned forces, the U.S. Army could become a significant influence in making the United States both a conciliator and balancer in the region.

U.S. ratification of UNCLOS is another important step to influence the evolution of future interpretations of freedom of navigation toward more open stipulations than some of the states around the South China Sea now espouse. Although a more difficult proposition, the United States should demand the clarification of the historic claims made in the South China Sea, in order to facilitate negotiating a settlement, accelerate economic development, and remove the potential of shutting down all foreign navigation through the region. Support to Vietnam's current islet occupations in the Spratlys, its claims to coastal EEZ and continental shelf areas in compliance with UNCLOS, and specific historic economic rights could wean Vietnam from its otherwise weak historic claims, and pursue U.S. policy that countries comply with generally accepted views of international law. The United States has less influence to change China's position on historic rights because the ambiguity of its positions has served China well. Here, appealing to China's future role in world politics may help to change its parochial freedom of navigation perspective into a more global one like the United States holds. The United States has several options in the region to preserve freedom of navigation in the South China Sea.

Open economic access to the South China Sea maritime commons is a second U.S. interest, but one which may diverge from freedom of navigation. Access to the resources of the high seas has been an important enough U.S. interest to stall the ratification of UNCLOS for nearly 20 years in order to avoid the restrictions imposed on seabed mining, although this activity has yet to become commercially viable. However, while the United States remains outside the treaty, it holds less influence over how maritime law is interpreted and evolves, and thus is at a disadvantage to shape events like whether the South China Sea becomes a wholly divided and claimed sea. Such arrangements as a Joint Development Zone or a Joint Management Zone could stabilize the area to provide stability and economic development for its participants. This could detract from potential U.S. economic development activities, depending on the arrangements, but supports U.S. security and economic prosperity goals for the region as well as attaining a diplomatic settlement through recognized international law.

Joint solutions could include a sharing arrangement through a Svalbard-like Spratly Islands Treaty in which the United States could participate, or shares in a Philippine administered archipelagic annexation from which the United States would be excluded. A different approach in which no sovereignty was awarded would follow the Antarctic Treaty model in which the Spratlys would be administered by an international authority, but the resulting diminution of bordering states' security and development interests in this choice makes it less viable. Any joint or shared solution would be more acceptable to the international community if outside states could also be a party to it, but the more inclusive a solution the less attractive it becomes to the PRC which sees itself as the original sole owner with a growing ability to enforce that claim. To support any of the joint solutions, the United States would have to place its security interests over potential economic ones.

To contribute to overall stability and prosperity in the region, and its own freedom of navigation and economic interests, the United States must delicately play the roles of conciliator and balancer as circumstances require. The United States is an honest broker through "active neutrality" because it shares goals in common with the states around the South China Sea, in accord with existing U.S. policy. Although the United States may not be truly neutral, it has less direct demands in the disputes, garners more trust than most other states, and possesses resources to bear on these problems, making it a useful interlocutor in resolving problems.

In other circumstances, the United States has intervened in problems around the Spratly Islands in more parochial ways to balance the diplomatic field in aid of allies and defense partners, and to directly protect its freedom of navigation interests in a policy some have dubbed "active concern." Just as the U.S. honest broker role limits the demands that its partners might make in the disputes, the balancer role should deter aggressive stances by any party lest the United States throw its weight to the other side. The balancer role is also dictated by U.S. treaty obligation to the Philippines, and because ASEAN lacks a defense arrangement by which to counter the influence of a much stronger PRC. As a balancer, the United States has improved ASEAN states' military capabilities and cooperation, and challenged Chinese actions which Chinese officials have complained "internationalizes" the issues. The balancing role should be minimal so as not to overshadow the conciliator role, since both are necessary roles that only the United States can play well in order to achieve the peaceful settlements toward security and economic interests that ultimately all the states want. In short, all parties should welcome a nuanced U.S. role as both conciliator, to keep the United States relatively neutral in the disputes, and balancer, to deter aggressive actions and thus support diplomatic solutions.

This monograph presented the most important economic, security, and diplomatic interests that the United States has in the region. Its involvement as described must be nuanced to balance conflicting requirements to ensure its freedom of navigation through these waters, which also reinforces similar rights around the world, and economic development interests. The balancer role ensures that allies and partners may represent themselves as full sovereign states in negotiations with each other, while the United States simultaneously maintains good economic and diplomatic relations with each of the claimant states as a conciliator. For these reasons, the United States has again made the Asia-Pacific region a major focus of its stated global interests, and converging national interests between the United States and China may indicate that some progress on the issues outlined here are possible.

The importance of the Spratly Islands region to world trade, energy, and security; the intricacy of the bitter problems involved; and its own interests require careful American involvement in this Dangerous Ground. To best address the disputes, policymakers must understand the underlying territorial and maritime claims of the PRC, Taiwan, Vietnam, Malaysia, Indonesia, Brunei, and the Philippines in order to help manage these issues peacefully and equitably for the regional states, and to meet U.S. interests. In the end, the conflict in the Spratly Islands is not one for the United States to solve, but its ability to contribute, facilitate, balance, or support is necessary to achieve a solution from which all may benefit.

ENDNOTES

1. Wanli Yu, "The American Factor in China's Maritime Strategy," Andrew S. Erickson, Lyle J. Goldstein, and Nan Li, eds., *China, the United States, and 2st Century Sea Power*, Newport, RI: Naval Institute Press, 2010, pp. 479-480.

2. Jon M. Van Dyke and Dale L. Bennet, "Islands and the Delimitation of Ocean Space in the South China Seas," Elisabeth Mann Borgese, Norton Ginsburg, and Joseph R. Morgan, eds., *Ocean Yearbook 10*, Chicago, IL: University of Chicago Press, 1993, p. 65; Chengxin Pan, "Is the South China Sea a New 'Dangerous Ground' for US-China Rivalry?" *EastAsiaForum*, May 24, 2011, available from *www.eastasiaforum.org/2011/05/24/is-the-south-china-sea-a-new-dangerous-ground-for-us-china-rivalry/*; and Mark J. Valencia, "The Spratly Islands: Dangerous Ground in the South China Sea," *Pacific Review*, Vol. 1, No. 4, 1988, p. 438.

3. The number of features counted in the South China Sea varies widely depending on the definitions used. The criteria includes whether a feature is exposed above sea level or not, but some are debated as marginal and could go either way. In this monograph, the term "features" casts a wide net over any piece of land close to or above the water surface that affects navigation. Terms like islands, islets, shoals, reefs, banks, cays, sands, and rocks are more technical geographic terms which are defined when needed for analysis. While Hong's count of 170 features is cited here, Greenfield cites 500 features, 100 of which have been named, and 20 are above sea level at high tide (Jeanette Greenfield, "China and the Law of the Sea," J. Crawford and D. R. Rothwell, eds., *The Law of the Sea in the Asia Pacific Region*, Boston, MA: Martinus Nijhoff Publishers, 1995, pp. 27-28), and Fravel counts 230 features in the Spratleys alone (M. Taylor Fravel, "Chapter II: Maritime Security in the South China Sea and the Competition over Maritime Rights," Patrick M. Cronin, ed., *Cooperation from Strength: The United States, China and the South China Sea*, Washington, DC: Center for a New American Security, January 2012, p. 34). David Lai reports 30,000 features in the Spratlys, with 50 considered as islands (David Lai, *The United States and China in Power Transition*, Carlisle, PA: Strategic Studies Institute, U.S. Army War College, 2011, p. 131). Such technicalities are important and much disputed since they influence island sovereignty and maritime claim issues. For ease of reference, the South China

Sea discussion herein does not include the waters south or west of the line drawn from southern most coastal Sarawak on Borneo to the southernmost point in Vietnam running through Indonesia's Natuna Basar (Island). This excludes Cambodia, Thailand, and Singapore from the discussion, but their influence is no greater in these particular disputes than other Southeast Asian states like Laos, Burma, or East Timor.

4. Nong Hong, *UNCLOS and Ocean Dispute Settlement: Law and Politics in the South China Sea*, New York: Routledge, 2011, pp. 55, 57; "South China Sea," Washington, DC: United States Energy Information Administration (USEIA), February 7, 2013, available from *www.eia.gov/countries/regions-topics.cfm?fips=SCS*; and Ben Dolven, Shirley A. Kan, and Mark E. Manyin, "Maritime Territorial Disputes in East Asia: Issues for Congress," Washington, DC: Congressional Research Service, January 30, 2013, available from *https:// www.hsdl.org/?view&did=730456*.

5. Greenfield, "China and the Law of the Sea," pp. 28, 34; Van Dyke and Bennett, p. 54; and "South China Sea," Map 737328, Washington, DC: Central Intelligence Agency (CIA), December 1995.

6. Mark J. Valencia, Jon M. Van Dyke, and Noel A. Ludwig, *Sharing the Resources of the South China Sea*, The Hague, The Netherlands: Martinus Nijhoff Publishers, 1997, p. 187.

7. Tom Ness, "Dangers to the Environment," Timo Kivimaki, ed., *War or Peace in the South China Sea?* Copenhagen, Denmark: Nordic Institute of Asian Studies Press, 2002, pp. 43-4; and Dolven, Kan, and Manyin, p. 20.

8. Note: Not all of the seafood reported here originated in the South China Sea, but this sea is a major source. International Crisis Group (ICG), "The South China Sea (II): Regional Responses," *Asia Report 229*, Beijing/Jakarta/Brussels: ICG, July 24, 2012, pp. 16-17, available from *www.crisisgroup.org/en/regions/asia/ north-east-asia/china/229-stirring-up-the-south-china-sea-ii-regional-responses.aspx*.

9. Hong, p. 220; and Valencia, Van Dyke, and Ludwig, p. 188.

10. Valencia, Van Dyke, and Ludwig, p. 188; ICG, "The South China Sea (II)," p. ii; and John C. Baker and David G. Wiencek, "Introduction," John C. Baker and David G. Wiencek, eds., *Cooperative Monitoring in the South China Sea: Satellite Imagery, Confidence-Building Measures, and the Spratly Islands Disputes*, Westport, CT: Praeger Publishers, 2002.

11. Fravel, p. 37; ICG, "The South China Sea (II)," p. 13; and James R. Clapper, "Statement for the Record, Worldwide Threat Assessment of the U.S. Intelligence Community," Washington, DC: Senate Select Committee on Intelligence, March 12, 2013, p. 10.

12. Robert D. Kaplan, "The Geography of Chinese Power. How Far Can Beijing Reach on Land and at Sea?" *Foreign Affairs*, Vol. 89, No. 3, May/Jun 2010, pp. 37-8; Hong, p. 5; and Pan.

13. "Spratly Islands," *The 2012 World Factbook*, Washington, DC: CIA, 2012, available from *https://www.cia.gov/library/publications/the-world-factbook/geos/ni.html*; Ramses Amer, "Ongoing Efforts in Conflict Management," Kivimaki, ed., p. 120; and Valencia, Van Dyke, and Ludwig, p. 10.

14. USEIA, "South China Sea."

15. In 2011, China ranks between 15th and 17th worldwide in proven oil reserves, and 13th in natural gas. However, as the world's largest consumer of energy, and second largest consumer of oil, it imports 57 percent of its oil and 29 percent of its natural gas, over half of both forms of energy transit the South China Sea. "China," Washington, DC: USEIA, September 4, 2012, available from *www.eia.gov/countries/country-data.cfm?fips=CH*; and CIA, "South China Sea."

16. Michael Studeman, "Calculating China's Advances in the South China Sea: Identifying the Triggers of Expansion," *Naval War College Review*, Vol. 51, No. 2, Spring 1998, available from *www.globalsecurity.org/military/library/report/1998/art5-sp8.htm*; and Andrew Higgins, "In South China Sea, a Dispute over Energy," *Washington Post*, September 7, 2011, available from *www.washingtonpost.com/world/asia-pacific/in-south-china-sea-a-dispute-over-energy/2011/09/07/gIQA0PrQaK_story.html*.

17. Valencia, Van Dyke, and Ludwig, pp. 9-10; and Stein Tonnesson, "The Economic Dimension: Natural Resources and Sea Lanes," Kivimaki, ed., pp. 56-57.

18. Hong, p. 75; and Dolven, Kan, and Manyin, p. 22.

19. ICG, "The South China Sea (II)," p. 15; Higgins; and USEIA, "South China Sea."

20. Hong, p. 66.

21. USEIA, "South China Sea."

22. ICG, "The South China Sea (II)," pp. 3, 33; Seth Robson, "China's Tactics Turning Off Asian Neighbors," *Stars and Stripes*, June 25, 2013, available from *www.military.com/daily-news/2013/06/25/chinas-tactics-turning-off-asian-neighbors.html?ESRC=airforce-a.nl*; and Ronald O. O'Rourke, *Maritime Territorial and Exclusive Economic Zone (EEZ) Disputes Involving China: Issues for Congress*, Washington, DC: Congressional Research Service, August 9, 2013, p. 25, available from *www.fas.org/sgp/crs/row/R42784.pdf*.

23. Fravel, p. 36. In part this is because the "involvement of non-claimants in joint exploration in the South China Sea also feeds Beijing's fears of containment," like the pact between Russia's Gazprom and PetroVietnam to explore two blocks on the Vietnamese continental shelf signed in April 2012, or joint exploration with India. ICG, "The South China Sea (II)," p. 33.

24. Hong, p. 186; Valencia, Van Dyke, and Ludwig, p. 9; ICG, "The South China Sea (II)," p. 33; and Dolven, Kan, and Manyin, p. 21.

25. Douglas H. Paal, "Territorial Disputes in Asian Waters," Washington, DC: Carnegie Endowment for International Peace, October 16, 2012, available from *carnegieendowment.org/2012/10/16/territorial-disputes-in-asian-waters/e1ez*; and ICG, "The South China Sea (II)," p. 14.

26. ICG, "The South China Sea (II)," p. 14.

27. *Ibid.*, p. 7.

28. Dolven, Kan, and Manyin, p. 20.

29. Hong, p. 57.

30. Stein Tonnesson, "The History of the Dispute," Kivimaki, ed., p. 7; Pan; and Van Dyke and Bennett, p. 65.

31. Hong, p. 7.

32. Christopher C. Joyner, "The Spratly Islands Dispute: Legal Issues and Prospects for Diplomatic Accommodation," Baker and Wiencek, eds.

33. Valencia, Van Dyke, and Ludwig, pp. 188, 230.

34. Ness, p. 43; Valencia, Van Dyke, and Ludwig, p. 179; and GlobalSecurity, "Spratly Islands Conflicting Claims," Alexandria, VA: GlobalSecurity.org, undated, available from *www.globalsecurity.org/military/world/war/spratly-conflict.htm*.

35. Timo Kivimaki, "Conclusion," Kivimaki, ed., p. 168.

36. *Ibid.*, p. 165.

37. Valencia, p. 438; Valencia, Van Dyke, and Ludwig, p. 7; and Van Dyke and Bennett, p. 67.

38. Lai, *The United States and China in Power Transition*, p. 213.

39. *Ibid.*, p. 136.

40. Rongsheng Ma, "Geostrategic Thinking on Land-and-Sea Integration," *China Military Science Journal*, Vol. 1, No. 1, 2012, p. 58.

41. Gabriel B. Collins, "China's Dependence on the Global Maritime Commons," Erickson, Goldstein, and Nan Li, eds., p. 21; Peter A. Dutton, "Charting the Course: Sino-American Naval Cooperation to Enhance Governance and Security," Erickson, Goldstein, and Nan Li, eds., p. 214; Michael D. Swaine and M.

Taylor Fravel, "China's Assertive Behavior – Part One: On 'Core Interests,'" *China Leadership Monitor*, Vol. 34, Winter 2011, pp. 7-9, available from *www.carnegieendowment.org/files/CLM34MS_FINAL.pdf*; and Kaplan.

42. Valencia, p. 440; and Valencia, Van Dyke, and Ludwig, p. 33.

43. Timo Kivimaki, "Introduction," Kivimaki, ed., p. 1.

44. Baker and Wiencek, eds., "Introduction"; CIA, "Spratly Islands"; Lai, *The United States and China in Power Transition* , p. 131; and Shicun Wu, "Opportunities and Challenges for China-US Cooperation in the South China Sea," Erickson, Goldstein, and Nan Li, eds., p. 366.

45. Van Dyke and Bennett, p. 64.

46. David G. Wiencek and John C. Baker, "Security Risks of a South China Sea Conflict," Baker and Wiencek, eds.; Joyner; and Dolven, Kan and Manyin, pp. 28-29.

47. Joyner; Wiencek and Baker, "Security Risks of a South China Sea Conflict"; Valencia, p. 439; and Baker and Wiencek, "Introduction."

48. Van Dyke and Bennett, pp. 74-75; Joyner; ICG, "The South China Sea (II)," p. 38; Fravel, p. 34; and Valencia, p. 440.

49. Valencia, Van Dyke, and Ludwig, p. 37; Joyner; Baker and Wiencek, "Introduction"; ICG, "The South China Sea (II)," p. 38; and Fravel, p. 34.

50. Joyner; Hong, p. 13; and Dolven, Kan, and Manyin, pp. 28-29.

51. Studeman.

52. Dolven, Kan, and Manyin, p. 9; Wiencek and Baker, "Security Risks of a South China Sea Conflict"; and Joyner.

53. Joyner; and Baker and Wiencek, "Introduction."

54. Joyner.

55. Timo Kivimaki, Liselotte Odgaard, and Stein Tonnesson, "What Could be Done?" Kivimaki, ed., *War or Peace in the South China Sea?* p. 149; Fravel, p. 34; and Wiencek and Baker, "Security Risks of a South China Sea Conflict."

56. Hong, p. 189.

57. Studeman; and Tonnesson, "The History of the Dispute," p. 15.

58. Greenfield, p. 30; and Yu, p. 474.

59. The number of Vietnamese killed in this action varies up to 120, and losses are reported between one and three vessels. No reliable numbers of Chinese deaths are confirmed or if any of its vessels were lost or damaged. This skirmish followed an earlier naval clash in 1974 between the Republic of Vietnam (then South Vietnam) and PRC forces over the Parcel Island archipelago in which several frigate and escort size vessels were reported sunk on both sides, with 53 Vietnamese and an unreported number of Chinese sailors killed. Adding to the animosity was a brief but intense border war in 1979 in which Vietnam suffered between 35,000 and 62,000 casualties, and China between 20,000 and 63,500. Joyner; Van Dyke and Bennett, p. 59; Fravel, pp. 35-36; and ICG, "The South China Sea (II)," pp. 2-3.

60. Studeman.

61. Wiencek and Baker, "Security Risks of a South China Sea Conflict."

62. Fravel, p. 36.

63. O'Rourke, *Maritime Territorial and Exclusive Economic Zone (EEZ) Disputes Involving China*, pp. 20, 23.

64. These are sometimes referred to as five "dragons stirring up the sea." The five maritime agencies include: Maritime Police of the Border Control Department (BCD), the largest and only armed agency; Maritime Safety Administration, the second

largest, under the Ministry of Transportation; Fisheries Law Enforcement Command (FLEC) under the Ministry of Agriculture; General Administration of Customs; and the Marine Surveillance Force (MSF) over pollution and science of the State Oceanic Administration. See Lyle J. Goldstein, "Improving Chinese Maritime Enforcement Capabilities," Erickson, Goldstein, and Nan Li, eds., p. 127; and Dolven, Kan, and Manyin, pp. 23-24.

65. This new organization appears to be modeled on the U.S. Coast Guard. Jane Perlez, "Chinese, with Revamped Force, Make Presence Known in East China Sea," *The New York Times*, July 28, 2013, p. A.9.

66. ICG, "The South China Sea (II)," p. 28.

67. O'Rourke, *Maritime Territorial and Exclusive Economic Zone (EEZ) Disputes Involving China*, pp. 20-21.

68. Fravel, p. 45. In 2011, no Vietnamese fishing ships were detained, although catches and equipment continued to be confiscated, showing how improvement in relations with Vietnam was reflected at sea, although this does not seem to have transferred over to the more sensitive energy exploration sector. During this time, however, enforcement against Filipino vessels worsened with the deterioration of relations between the two. Relations between Malaysia and the PRC have generally remained good, which, when combined with the distance between the two countries, explains why there are few incidents between them. ICG, "The South China Sea (II)," p.11.

69. ICG, "The South China Sea (II)," pp. 4-7; Fravel, p. 38; and Hong, p. 31.

70. The incident was over the boarding and confiscation of illegal shark and coral finds on Chinese fishing vessels by the Filipino coast guard. The incident also involved Chinese Marine Surveillance Agency vessels and a Filipino warship, although the latter was quickly withdrawn and the government publicly admitted that was an inappropriate use of that vessel. The PRC retaliated by restricting imports of Filipino fruits into China and warning its tourists against travel to the Philippines. The ultimate Chinese motive behind the standoff was to demonstrate effective Chinese administrative control in its claim and occupation of the

shoals. Dolven, Kan, and Manyin, pp. 23, 25; and ICG, "The South China Sea (II)," pp. 8-9, 28.

71. O'Rourke, *Maritime Territorial and Exclusive Economic Zone (EEZ) Disputes Involving China*, pp. 23-24.

72. *Ibid.*, p. 27.

73. ICG, "The South China Sea (II)," p. ii.

74. Robson.

75. O'Rourke, *Maritime Territorial and Exclusive Economic Zone (EEZ) Disputes Involving China*, p. 23.

76. Hong, pp. 21, 74; and Valencia, Van Dyke, and Ludwig, pp. 98-99.

77. Valencia, p. 439.

78. Amer, "Ongoing Efforts in Conflict Management," p. 128.

79. ICG, "The South China Sea (II)," p. ii.

80. Fravel, p. 38.

81. Only Brunei seems exempt from this melee since it does not occupy any of its claimed geologic features nor does it actively patrol its small maritime claim. Incidents between Malaysia and the PRC are also relatively few, perhaps in part due to the greater distance between them than is true for the PRC in relation to the Philippines and Vietnam, and because Malaysia seems to have struck an informal understanding with China. Reports of incidents between ASEAN states and Taiwan are rare, and may be because of a greater discipline that Taiwan may impose on its fishing fleet due to its more tentative international standing and need to cultivate friends. However, one such incident occurred in May 2013 when the Philippine Coast Guard killed a Taiwanese fisherman in disputed waters. In retaliation, Taiwan imposed economic sanctions on the Philippines, froze visas on Filipino workers, and conducted naval drills in the Bashi Channel between the two parties. Valencia, Van Dyke, and Ludwig, p. 9; Dolven, Kan, and Manyin, pp. 11-12; Hong, p. 74; Valencia, p. 438; ICG,

"The South China Sea (II)," pp. ii, 2; and Ashish Kuman Sen, "Taiwan-Philippines Dispute Erupts after Fisherman's Killing," *The Washington Times*, May 20, 2012, available from *www.washingtontimes.com/news/2013/may/20/taiwan-philippines-dispute-erupts-after-fishermans/?page=all.*

82. Fravel, p. 38.

83. Ramses Amer and Timo Kivimaki, "The Political Dimension: Sources of Conflict and Stability," Kivimaki, ed., p. 89.

84. Hong, p. 21; Studeman; and Bjorn Moller, "The Military Aspects of the Disputes," Kivimaki, ed., p. 77.

85. Dolven, Kan, and Manyin, p. i; ICG, "The South China Sea (II)," p. iii.

86. USEIA, "South China Sea." In 2004, 74 percent of Chinese oil imports originated from the Middle East or Africa, and most of that transited the South China Sea en route to Chinese ports. As the Chinese economy grows and its domestic production levels, this number has since grown. Over half of China's oil and over a quarter of its natural gas was imported in 2011. CIA, *World Factbook,* "China"; Daojiong Zha, "China's Energy Security and Its International Relations," *The China and Eurasia Forum Quarterly,* Vol. 3, No. 3, November 2005, p. 49; and Ingolf Kiesow, *China's Quest for Energy: Impact upon Foreign and Security Policy,* Stockholm, Sweden: Swedish Defence Research Agency, November 2004, pp. 12-15.

87. Wiencek and Baker, "Security Risks of a South China Sea Conflict"; Pan; and Hong, p. 5.

88. Fravel, p. 35; Greenfield, p. 26; and CIA, "South China Sea" map.

89. *USPACOM Strategy,* Camp Smith, HI: U.S. Pacific Command, January 22, 2013, p. 2.

90. Baker and Wiencek, "Introduction."

91. Fravel, pp. 33-34.

92. Van Dyke and Bennett, p. 88; and Shicun Wu, p. 368.

93. Japan, for instance, is militarily able to project naval power into the South China Sea but is politically hobbled by its constitution and historical enmity after World War II to play a direct role in the region. See Wiencek and Baker, "Security Risks of a South China Sea Conflict." South Korea's naval force projection is limited, and needed closer to home to protect against an erratic North Korea. Taiwan's navy is capable and in close proximity, but in times of increased friction in the region would be needed to defend the homeland, and Taiwan is not diplomatically recognized by any of the other claimant states. The Philippines is militarily weak, and relies heavily on its defense alliance with the United States to maintain its security. Other states see the U.S. presence as a counterbalance to a militarily strong and actively involved PRC.

94. Fravel, p. 42; and Kivimaki, Odgaard, and Tonnesson, p. 141.

95. Robson.

96. Roger Baker, "China Tests Japanese and US Patience," Austin, TX: STRATFOR, February 26, 2013, available from *www.stratfor. com/weekly/china-tests-japanese-and-us-patience?utm_source=freelist-f&utm_medium=email&utm_campaign=20130226&utm_term=gweekly&utm_content=readmore&elq=8c6ebca11e10439b995e3 aa98be897d4.*

97. Fravel, p. 33; and Kaplan.

98. Pan; Erikson and Goldstein, "Introduction," Erickson, Goldstein, and Nan Li, eds., p. xiii; and Ronald O. O'Rourke. *China Naval Modernization: Implications for U.S. Navy Capabilities – Background and Issues for Congress*, Washington, DC: Congressional Research Service, December 10, 2012, p. i, available from *www.fas.org/sgp/crs/row/RL33153.pdf.*

99. Valencia, Van Dyke, and Ludwig, p. 2; and Kivimaki, "Introduction," p. 1.

100. David N. Griffiths, "Challenges in the Development of Military-to-Military Relationships," Erickson, Goldstein, and Nan Li, eds., pp. 38-39.

101. Bloomberg News, "China Streamlines Maritime Law Enforcement Amid Island Disputes," Bloomberg News Services, March 10, 2013, available from *www.bloomberg.com/news/2013-03-10/china-bolsters-maritime-law-enforcement-amid-island-disputes. html*; and Valencia, Van Dyke, and Ludwig, p. 131.

102. O'Rourke, *China Naval Modernization*, p. 8. The ROC and Vietnam also make similarly wide claims to all of the South China Sea, but have not enforced them, as has the PRC.

103. Dolven, Kan, and Manyin, p. 5.

104. O'Rourke, *China Naval Modernization*, p. 8; ICG, "The South China Sea (II)," p. 18; and O'Rourke, *Maritime Territorial and EEZ Disputes*, p. 4.

105. Lai, *The United States and China in Power Transition*, p. 120; and O'Rourke, *China Naval Modernization*, p. 8.

106. ICG, "The South China Sea (II)," p. 18; Fravel, p. 35; and Hong, pp. 30-32.

107. Matthew Lee, "US Takes Aim at China, Ups Naval Aid to SE Asia," Associated Press, December 16, 2013, available from *news.yahoo.com/us-takes-aim-china-ups-naval-aid-se-105727402--politics.html <http://news.yahoo.com/us-takes-aim-china-ups-naval-aid-se-105727402--politics.html.*

108. Hong, p. 94.

109 . Fravel, p. 34; and Ivan Shearer, "Navigation Issues in the Asian Pacific Region," Crawford and Rothwell, eds., p. 219.

110. Valencia, Van Dyke, and Ludwig, p. 17; and Hong, p. 58.

111. Hong, p. 222.

112. *Ibid.*, p. 93; and Van Dyke and Bennett, p. 89.

113. Hong, p. 223.

114. Joyner.

115. Hong, pp. 42, 54-55.

116. Or more like adding apples and oranges. Since the imposition of the Treaty Port System in 1842, however, Asian societies have had to assimilate European imposed international customary law in order to compete successfully to retain or gain land. Van Dyke and Bennett, pp. 62-63; and Kivimaki, "Conclusion," p. 126.

117. Hong, pp. 109-110.

118. ICG, "The South China Sea (II)," p. 29.

119. Hong, p. 54; and Shicun Wu, p. 365.

120. Kivimaki, Odgaard, and Tonnesson, p. 154.

121. The International Law Commission in 1962 outlined the criteria for exercising authority over an historic area as the continuous exercise of that authority and repeated use of the area, and acceptance of these by other states in *Juridical Regime of Historic Waters, Including Historic Bays*, Valencia, Van Dyke, and Ludwig, p. 26; Van Dyke and Bennett, p. 80; and Shearer, p. 208.

122. Hong, p. 66; and Valencia, Van Dyke, and Ludwig, p. 26.

123. Hong, p. 16; and Lai, *The United States and China in Power Transition*, pp. 127-128.

124. Valencia, Van Dyke, and Ludwig, p. 66; and Hong, pp. 66, 70-71.

125. Hong, pp. 63, 130.

126. Valencia, Van Dyke, and Ludwig, p. 25; and Hong, pp. 64-65.

127. ICG, "The South China Sea (II)," p. 29.

128. Wiencek and Baker, "Security Risks of a South China Sea Conflict."

129. Despite their many other disagreements, the PRC and ROC both assert identical historic and other claims to the South China Sea based on the same historic evidence. This mutual position could be termed "China's" or the "Chinese" claim, terms which this monograph will employ as pertaining to both unless otherwise noted. See Joyner; Ramses Amer, "Claims and Conflict Situations," Kivimaki, ed., p. 34. Although this claim was first formally proclaimed by the ROC in 1947, it was echoed by the PRC in 1951 by claiming sovereignty over the Paracel and Spratly Islands, and in 1958 over maritime rights. These claims were formally reiterated in PRC law in 1992 and 1998, and diplomatically in 2009. See Fravel, p. 41. Both parties have periodically and recently reasserted their historic claim to the South China Sea. This area of common interest has offered interesting opportunities for both sides to work together including joint oceanographic expeditions, economic development schemes, and the only representation by both parties in multilateral negotiations, the Indonesian sponsored Track II talks which includes each of the South China Sea claimants. See Hong, p. 211; Tonnesson, "The History of the Dispute," p. 19. Taiwanese participation in international fora is otherwise proscribed under the PRC's "one China policy." Although the claims are the same for both, the Taiwanese government has rarely asserted them as boldly or physically as has the PRC. ICG, "The South China Sea (II)," pp. 1, 12, 30, 36; Valencia, Van Dyke, and Ludwig, p. 96; Greenfield, p. 33; and Dolvern, Kan, and Manyin, p. 10.

130. USEIA, "South China Sea"; Hong, p. 17; ICG, "The South China Sea (II)," p. 37.

131. ICG, "The South China Sea (II)," p. 37; Valencia, Van Dyke, and Ludwig, p. 30; Shicun Wu, p. 366; Van Dyke and Bennett, p. 68.

132. ICG, "The South China Sea (II)," p. 37; Hong, p. 17.

133. Vietnam refers to the South China Sea as the "East Sea," and the Chinese use the name "South Sea." The Philippines be-

gan referring to it as the "West Philippine Sea" in 2011 to reinforce its own claim and undercut that of the Chinese. See Dona Pazzibugan and Norman Bordadora, "'It's West Philippine Sea' Gov't, AFP Use It Now to Refer to Disputed Spratly Area," *Philippine Daily Inquirer*, June 11, 2011, available from *newsinfo. inquirer.net/13833/%e2%80%98it%e2%80%99s-west-philippine-sea%e2%80%99*. Throughout this monograph, the standard names used by the U.S. Board on Geographic Names is employed for consistency.

134. Hong, p. 69.

135. Dr. David Lai, Interview on February 21, 2013, at Carlisle Barracks, PA.

136. Valencia, Van Dyke, and Ludwig, p. 32; and Hong, p. 17.

137. Hong pp. 6-7; and Tonnenson, "The History of the Dispute," p. 8.

138. Hong, p. 12; and Valencia, Van Dyke, and Ludwig, p. 21.

139. Tonnenson, "The History of the Dispute," p. 16; and Hong p. 17.

140. Although Vietnam, the PRC, and the ROC all claim the Paracel and Spratly Islands in their entirety, along with Malaysia, the Philippines, and Brunei who partially claim the Spratleys, Vietnam does not claim Macclesfield Bank or Scarborough Shoal which lie further to the east or north of those island groups. The Philippines, however, does dispute both of these geologic features with the Chinas. Lai, *The United States and China in Power Transition*, p. 131.

141. Valencia, Van Dyke, and Ludwig, p. 25; USEIA, "South China Sea"; Lai, *The United States and China in Power Transition*, p. 222; and Dolven, Kan, and Manyin, p. 6. Taiwan codified its historic waters claim to the region within its U-shaped line in 1993 in its *South China Sea Policy Guidelines*. Hong, p. 68.

142. Greenfield, pp. 21-22; and Hong, p. 16.

143. Dolven, Kan, and Manyin, p. 8; and Hong, p. 16.

144. Valencia, Van Dyke, and Ludwig, p. 21; and Tonnenson, "History of the Dispute," p. 9.

145. Hong, p. 16.

146. Hong, p. 101. It is worth noting that the present Law of the Sea treaty categorizes islands as above the water at high tide, not the low water tide method cited here by the Chinese. Hong, p. 50.

147. Hong, p. 68; and ICG, "The South China Sea (II)," p. 36.

148. Such ambiguity has been consistent and probably purposeful, since it allows flexibility on the Chinese side and has made negotiations for the other claimants more difficult. The Chinese claim was originally drawn with 11-dash lines, but revised to 9-dash lines in 1953 when two were removed in the Gulf of Tonkin without explanation. Some observers feel that the use of a dashed line rather than a solid one also indicates the claim is subject to change, and China and Vietnam bilaterally negotiated a partial maritime border in the Gulf of Tonkin in 2000. See ICG, "The South China Sea (II)," p. 36; Fravel, pp. 41-42; and Dolven, Kan, and Manyin, p. 8. In 2012, a PRC foreign ministry spokesperson may have indicated some clarification in stating, "No country including China has claimed sovereignty over the entire South China Sea" and that China's claims in the 9-dash line were for land features and not to the entire water area. See ICG, "The South China Sea (II)," p. 4. Promising though such a statement seems for transparency, internal rifts within the government may "clarify" the position differently later, continuing the ambiguity to its claim. Although diplomatically useful, in negotiations a vague claim may weaken its legal status, since historic claims should be well-known and understood by other countries in order for them to be recognized as Chinese. Valencia, Van Dyke, and Ludwig, p. 27.

149. Greenfield, p. 32; Van Dyke and Bennett, pp. 63-64; and Hong, p. 16.

150. Greenfield, pp. 29-30; and Tonnesson, "History of the Dispute," p. 7.

151. "Vietnam Refuses to Stamp New Chinese Passport," AFP, November 27, 2012, available from *www.google.com/hosted-news/afp/article/ALeqM5jf38Wx8pQuvIrgm:rwcibPlxqOzQg?docId=C NG.fd699e45805ce0638bbada0e1806e749.71*; and Robert Sutter and Chin Hao Huang, "China-Southeast Asia Relations: Managing Rising Tension in the South China Sea," *Comparative Connections*, Vol. 13, No. 2, September 2011, pp. 67-78, see especially p. 68.

152. Van Dyke and Bennett, pp. 62-63.

153. Valencia, Van Dyke, and Ludwig, pp. 22-24; and Hong, pp. 16, 64.

154. Lai, *The United States and China in Power Transition*, pp. 129, 221; and Fravel, p. 34.

155. Robson.

156. Valencia, Van Dyke, and Ludwig, pp. 26-27; Hong, p. 70; and Lai, *The United States and China in Power Transition*, p. 140.

157. Hong, pp. 68-69, 116.

158. Valencia, Van Dyke, and Ludwig, p. 39.

159. The Netherlands, on behalf of its colony, the Dutch East Indies (today Indonesia), and the United States for its possession of the Philippines, disputed the status of this Philippine Sea island just southeast of Mindanao. The United States based its claimed sovereignty in terms of discovery, inchoate title, while the Netherlands argued and won based on occupation and effective administration (prescriptive occupation). This case established a long standing principle that occupation takes precedence over discovery and historic claims. Later rulings by the International Court of Justice in 1953 in the Minquiers and Echreos Case between Great Britain and France over two groups of islets by Jersey, and the Gulf of Fonseca case by the same court in 1992 that awarded El Tigre island to Honduras are based on the same principle. Valencia, Van Dyke, and Ludwig, p. 17.

160. Lai, *The United States and China in Power Transition*, p. 221.

161. Valencia, Van Dyke, and Ludwig, pp. 28, 39; and ICG, "The South China Sea (II)," p. 30.

162. Valencia, Van Dyke, Ludwig, p. 37.

163. "Res Nullius Law & Legal Definition," USLegal, available from *definitions.uslegal.com/r/res-nullius/. Res nullis* may be equated to property without an owner because it is abandoned, which is slightly different from another Latin term also derived from Roman law, *terra nullis* ("land belonging to no one"), land without an owner because it is newly discovered, "has never been subject to the sovereignty of any state, or over which any prior sovereign has expressly or implicitly relinquished sovereignty." See "Terra Nullius Law & Legal Definition," USLegal, available from *definitions.uslegal.com/t/terra-nullius/*. Through *res nullis* property that is previously known and perhaps once claimed or occupied but subsequently not in use or abandoned, can be claimed and occupied to establish sovereignty over that land. Because the ownership claims to the Spratly Islands over the years have been overlapping and difficult to determine, this monograph uses the term *res nullis* for the status of the Spratly Islands when that claim is made by one of the powers involved. In terms of establishing sovereignty, there is little difference between a feature being occupied using one form or the other, as long as the occupation is effective.

164. Joyner; and Valencia, Van Dyke, and Ludwig, pp. 19-20.

165. Lai, *The United States and China in Power Transition*, pp. 130-131.

166. Greenfield, pp. 29-30.

167. Hong, p. 10; and Amer, "Claims and Conflict Situations," pp. 27-28.

168. Van Dyke and Bennett, pp. 64-65; and Hong, pp. 10, 17.

169. "Taiping Island," *Wikipedia*, available from *en.wikipedia.org/wiki/Taiping_(island)*.

170. Fravel, p. 41.

171. British Broadcasting Corporation (BBC), "Q&A: South China Sea Dispute," *BBC News Asia*, January 22, 2013, available from *www.bbc.co.uk/news/world-asia-pacific-13748349*; and ICG, "The South China Sea (II)," p. 5.

172. Dolven, Kan, and Manyin, p. 7; Wiencek and Baker, "Security Risks of a South China Sea Conflict"; and Valencia, Van Dyke, and Ludwig, p. 41.

173. Hong, p. 10.

174. Studeman.

175. Valencia, Van Dyke, and Ludwig, p. 23.

176. Lai, *The United States and China in Power Transition*, p. 133.

177. Douglas H. Paal, "Dangerous Shoals: US Policy in the South China Sea," Washington, DC: Carnegie Endowment for International Peace, August 11, 2012, available from *carnegieendowment.org/2012/08/11/dangerous-shoals-u.s.-policy-in-south-china-sea/dc0c*; and BBC, "Q&A: South China Sea Dispute."

178. Hong, p. 17.

179. Tonnesson, "The History of the Dispute," p. 10; Hong, p. 10; Shicun Wu, p. 365; and Greenfield, pp. 28-29.

180. Joyner.

181. Greenfield, pp. 32-33; and Hong, p. 13.

182. Tonnesson, "History of the Dispute," p. 17; and Joyner.

183. Swaine and Fravel, pp. 15-16; and Shicun Wu, p. 374.

184. Dolven, Kan, and Manyin, p. 11.

185. Shicun Wu, p. 365.

186. Tonnesson, "History of the Dispute," p. 11.

187. *Ibid.*, p. 12.

188. Van Dyke and Bennett, p. 72.

189. Tonnesson, "History of the Dispute," p. 13.

190. Shicun Wu, p. 368; Valencia, Van Dyke, and Ludwig, p. 33; Greenfield, p. 33; and Hong p. 18.

191. Joyner.

192. Hong, p. 12; and Tonnesson, "History of the Dispute," p. 13.

193. Hong, p. 13; and Van Dyke and Bennett, pp. 74-75.

194. Hong, p. 18; and Valencia, Van Dyke, and Ludwig, pp. 33-35.

195. Hong, p. 12; and Tonnesson, "History of the Dispute," p. 11.

196. Tonnesson, "History of the Dispute," p. 13; and Van Dyke and Bennett, pp. 68-69.

197. Hong, pp. 18-19; and Valencia, Van Dyke, and Ludwig, p. 35.

198. Valencia, Van Dyke, and Ludwig, p. 17; and Lai, "*The United States and China in Power Transition*, p. 221.

199. Lai, *The United States and China in Power Transition*, p. 128.

200. Van Dyke and Bennett, p. 65; Tonnesson, "History of the Dispute," p. 9; and Hong, p. 7.

201. Hong, p. 7.

202. Van Dyke and Bennett, p. 66; and Hong, p. 10.

203. Valencia, Van Dyke, and Ludwig, p. 37; Joyner; ICG, "The South China Sea (II)," p. 38; and Hong, p. 20.

204. Valencia, Van Dyke, and Ludwig, p. 37; and ICG, "The South China Sea (II)," p. 38.

205. Dolven, Kan, and Manyin, p. 13.

206. CIA, "South China Sea" Map; Dolven, Kan, and Manyin, p. 13; USEIA, "South China Sea"; ICG, "The South China Sea (II)," p. 38; Fravel, pp. 36-37; and Amer and Kivimaki, p. 101.

207. Valencia, Van Dyke, and Ludwig, p. 37; and Hong, p. 20.

208. Hong, p. 58.

209. ICG, "The South China Sea (II), p. ii.

210. Lai, *The United States and China in Power Transition*, p. 133.

211. "Uti Possidetis Law & Legal Definition," USLegal, available from *definitions.uslegal.com/u/uti-possidetis/*; and *"Uti Possidetis,"* Wikipedia, available from *en.wikipedia.org/wiki/Uti_possidetis*.

212. Lai, *The United States and China in Power Transition*, p. 140.

213. Sam Bateman, "Good Order at Sea in the South China Sea," Shicun Wu and Keyuan Zou, eds., *Maritime Security in the South China Sea: Regional Implication and International Cooperation*, Surrey, UK: Ashgate Publishing Limited, 2009, p. 29.

214. Anthony Bergin, "The High Seas Regime—Pacific Trends and Developments," Crawford and Rothwell, eds., *The Law of the Sea in the Asia Pacific Region*, pp. 183-185.

215. Bateman, p. 29.

216. Hong, pp. 46, 96; and Dolven, Kan, and Manyin, p. 31.

217. Christine Chinkin, "Dispute Resolution and the Law of the Sea: Regional Problems and Prospects," Crawford and Rothwell, eds., *The Law of the Sea in the Asia Pacific Region*, p. 248.

218. Hong, pp. 43-46, 72.

219. ICG, "The South China Sea (II)," p. 29.

220. Bergin, p. 195.

221. *United Nations Convention on the Law of the Sea,* New York: UN, Division for Ocean Affairs and the Law of the Sea, December 10, 1982, p. 63. (Hereafter UN *UNCLOS*)

222 . Hong, p. 51.

223. Valencia, Van Dyke, and Ludwig, pp. 41-42.

224. *Ibid.,* p. 40; and Bergin, p. 196.

225. Joyner; and Greenfield, p. 29.

226. See *Advisory Opinion on Western Sahara,* 1975; Valencia, Van Dyke, and Ludwig, p. 61.

227. Hong, p. 52.

228. Bergin, p. 196.

229. Valencia, Van Dyke, and Ludwig, pp. 41-42; and Van Dyke and Bennett, p. 89.

230. Valencia, Van Dyke, and Ludwig, p. 43; and Van Dyke and Bennett, pp. 78-79.

231. Van Dyke and Bennett, p. 75.

232. Hong, pp. 51-52; and Van Dyke and Bennett, p. 79.

233. Van Dyke and Bennett, pp. 81, 84-85. In 1978, for instance, the International Court of Justice awarded the Isles of Scilly, consisting of six small inhabited British islands in a group of 48 off the coast of Cornwall, only half of their jurisdiction against the maritime zones of France's Brittany Peninsula — deemed the "half effect." This concept was derived from an earlier negotiated settlement between Italy and Yugoslavia. Van Dyke and Bennett, p. 82.

234. These decisions were formed through the International Court of Justice rulings in the Tunisia-Libya Continental Shelf Case in 1982. The islands were given circular enclaves of 12-nm territorial water, and the rest of the surrounding maritime zone went to the continental state. Van Dyke and Bennett, pp. 83-86.

235. Van Dyke and Bennett, p. 77; and Hong, p 243.

236. Baker and Wiencek, "Introduction."

237. *Ibid.*

238. Van Dyke and Bennett, p. 89.

239. Dolven, Kan, and Manyin, p. 33.

240. Greenfield, p. 29; Valencia, Van Dyke, and Ludwig, p. 230; and Hong p. 59.

241. Valencia, Van Dyke, and Ludwig, pp. 44, 48.

242. Greenfield, p. 38.

243. Valencia, Van Dyke, and Ludwig, p. 56.

244. Dutton, p. 204; and UN, *UNCLOS*, p. 70.

245. The bay can be no wider than 24-nm between its entrance points. The line connecting the two entrance points becomes the territorial straight baseline. UN, *UNCLOS*, p. 28; and Shearer, p. 208.

246. UN, *UNCLOS*, p. 28.

247. "Maritime Claims of Northeast Asia," Map 772221AI, Washington, DC: CIA, July 2006; CIA, "South China Sea" Map; Jin-Hyun Paik, "East Asia and the Law of the Sea," Crawford and Rothwell, eds., *The Law of the Sea in the Asian Pacific Region*, p. 8; Tonnesson, "History of the Dispute," p. 15; and Hong, pp. 51, 127. Under their baseline proclamation, Vietnam can claim internal waters of 27,000 square nm with 9 of the 11 base points on islands ranging from 7.6-nm to 80.7-nm from shore. Hong, pp. 130-131.

248. UN, *UNCLOS,* p. 28.

249. Valencia, Van Dyke, and Ludwig, p. 26.

250. UN, *UNCLOS,* pp. 40-43; and Joyner.

251. UN, *UNCLOS,* p. 40; and Shearer, p. 204.

252. UN, *UNCLOS,* p. 40.

253. Greenfield, pp. 37-38.

254. Valencia, Van Dyke, and Ludwig, p. 47. UNCLOS allows an exception for up to 3 percent of the archipelagic base lines used to measure between 100 and 125-nm. See UN, *UNCLOS,* p. 40. Dr. Prescott's proposal would require three baselines measuring 107, 119, and 120-nm, and a relatively simple fix to increase the present 80 baselines used to define the Philippines sovereign maritime boundary to at least 100 baselines to comply with the 3 percent rule. See Valencia, Van Dyke, and Ludwig, p. 47; and ICG, "The South China Sea (II)," pp. 19, 38. In another notable exception from the rest of UNCLOS, Article 47 allows the use of drying reefs, land features exposed only at low tide, when determining archipelagic baselines, which are provisions Dr. Prescott employs in his work. See UN, *UNCLOS,* pp. 29, 40.

255. ICG, "The South China Sea (II)," pp. 19, 38; and Valencia, Van Dyke, and Ludwig, p. 48. Option 4 of this bill, to include Kalaya'an and Scarborough Shoal within the Philippine archipelago, required 135 baselines, with 4 between 100 and 125-nm long. This proposal was House Bill 3216, but was not accepted in the final Republic Act 5446. To complete an archipelagic claim under Bill 3216, UNCLOS would have required building lighthouses on the low tide elevation features at Sabina Shoal and Iroquois Reef. The practical obstacle to adding the Kalaya'an to the Philippines was that seven base points in this scheme are currently occupied by the PRC, Vietnam, or Malaysia. As Philippine Senator Trillanes concluded:

> contravention of the 2002 ASEAN-China Declaration on the Conduct of Parties in the South China Sea . . . may cause

outrage among affected States. Designating base points on uninhabited, though contested areas such as Scarborough Shoal can be defended legally and politically. But to place base points on foreign-occupied territory, no matter how strong our claim, is an act of aggression.

The Philippines was under pressure from an already extended international deadline to establish its archipelagic baseline in order to also make a continental shelf claim in accordance with UNCLOS. This forced them to draw the current baseline without Kalaya'an, but not to give up the Spratlys or a future archipelagic claim for them. Antonio F. Trillanes IV, "The Baseline Issue: A Position Paper," Manila, Philippines: Congress of the Philippines, undated, circa 2008, pp. 4, 6, 9, available from *verafiles.org/docs/trillanes-position-paper.pdf.*

256. Chinkin, p. 238; and Hong, p. 18.

257. UN, *UNCLOS,* pp. 29, 30.

258. Hong, p. 62.

259. Shearer, p. 208; and Valencia, Van Dyke, and Ludwig, p. 28.

260. Shearer, p. 208; and Hong, pp. 64-65.

261. Hong, pp. 60, 64, 67; and ICG, "The South China Sea (II)," pp. 29-30.

262. Hong, p. 71.

263. Valencia, Van Dyke, and Ludwig, p. 28.

264. ICG, "The South China Sea (II)," p. 36.

265. Amer, "Claims and Conflict Situations," pp. 30-31.

266. UN, *UNCLOS,* pp. 35, 66; Valencia, Van Dyke, and Ludwig, p. 47; and Under Secretary of Defense for Policy, *Maritime Claims Reference Manual, DoD 2005.1-M,* Washington, DC: Department of Defense, June 23, 2005, pp. 126-127, 690, available from *www.jag.navy.mil/organization/documents/mcrm/vietnam.pdf.*

267. Joyner; Dutton, p. 202-203; and Shicun Wu and Keyuan Zou, "Maritime Security in the South China Sea: Cooperation and Implications," Shicun Wu and Keyuan Zou, eds., *Maritime Security in the South China Sea: Regional Implication and International Cooperation*, Surrey, UK: Ashgate Publishing Limited, 2009, p. 5.

268. UN, *UNCLOS*, p. 31; and Hong, p. 72.

269. UN, *UNCLOS*, p. 33; and Shearer, p. 211.

270. UN, *UNCLOS*, p. 35; Dutton, p. 203; and Wu and Zou, pp. 4-5.

271. Paik, p. 12; and Shearer, p. 206.

272. UN, *UNCLOS*, p. 30.

273. Dutton, pp. 210-211; USEIA, "South China Sea"; Shearer, pp. 211, 219; and *UNCLOS Declarations and Statements*. New York: UN, Division for Ocean Affairs and the Law of the Sea, October 14, 1996, Malaysia Articles 2-4, available from *www.un.org/depts/los/convention_agreements/convention_declarations.htm#Malaysia*.

274. Hong, p. 132; and Dolven, Kan, and Manyin, p. 32.

275. Paik, p. 10; and Hong, p. 128.

276. Erikson and Goldstein, p xvii; Guifang Xue, "China and the Law of the Sea: A Sino-US Maritime Cooperation Perspective," Erickson, Goldstein, and Nan Li, eds., p. 176; and Dutton, p. 211.

277. Paik, p. 11; Greenfield, p. 30; Xue, p. 177; and Wiencek and Baker, "Security Risks of a South China Sea Conflict."

278. Hong, p. 114; Xue, p. 176; and UN, *UNCLOS Declarations and Statements*, China Article 4.

279. Hong, p. 110; Wiencek and Baker, "Security Risks of a South China Sea Conflict"; Studeman; and Swaine and Fravel, p. 7.

280. UN, *UNCLOS*, pp. 43-44.

281. Dutton, p. 203; UN, *UNCLOS*, pp. 43-44; and Wu and Zou, p. 5.

282. Shearer, p. 221; and UN, *UNCLOS*, pp. 44-49.

283. Shicun Wu, p. 366; and Bateman, "Good Order at Sea in the South China Sea," p. 29.

284. Davor Vidas, "The UN Convention on the Law of the Sea, the European Union, and the Rule of Law," Sanford Silverburg, ed., *International Law*, Boulder, CO: Westview Press, 2011, p. 340.

285. *1958 Geneva Conventions on the Law of the Sea*, Geneva, Switzerland: UN International Law Commission, April 29, 1958, p. 316, available from *untreaty.un.org/cod/avl/ha/gclos/gclos.html*; and Valencia, Van Dyke, and Ludwig, pp. 49-50.

286. Valencia, Van Dyke, and Ludwig, p. 135.

287. Hong, p. 60. The decision by the International Court of Justice awarding Britain's Channel Islands only territorial waters against the consideration of an entire EEZ to nearby continental France, and the St Pierre et Miquelon case, awarding the EEZ to Canada and not the tiny French possessions off its coast. Hong, p. 60; and Van Dyke and Bennett, p. 82.

288. Valencia, Van Dyke, and Ludwig, pp. 50-51.

289. Greenfield, p. 36.

290. Valencia, Van Dyke, and Ludwig, p. 48.

291. Amer, "Claims and Conflict Situation," p. 29; Valencia, Van Dyke, and Ludwig, p. 31; Greenfield, p. 32; CIA, *World Factbook*, pp. "Malaysia," "Philippines," "Vietnam," "Brunei"; CIA, "South China Sea" Map. Although the claims from the Philippine islands and Malaysian Borneo are indeed from islands, some scholars have asserted that they are "outlying components of the Asian continental margin, shielding the Asian marginal seas from the Pacific, and constitute out riding frontiers of the mainland

against the abyssal Pacific Ocean floor." This implies that both the Malaysian and Filipino coasts would have equal weighting with continental mainland coastlines when overlaps are delimitated using the equitable principle based on the ICJ's 1969 *North Sea Continental Shelf* cases. Greenfield, p. 34.

292. Valencia, Van Dyke, and Ludwig, p. 31; ICG, "The South China Sea (II)," p. 29. In a promising sign for resolving overlapping claims, China and Vietnam signed a delineation agreement settling disputes in the Tonkin Gulf along with a fishing protocol in 2000 that took effect in 2004. See also Hong, pp. 73, 127.

293. Valencia, Van Dyke, and Ludwig, pp. 55, 146; UN, *UNCLOS*, p. 57; Hong, p. 59; and CIA, "South China Sea" Map.

294. USIEA, "South China Seas"; and ICG, "The South China Sea (II)," p. 38.

295. Hong, p. 20; Valencia, Van Dyke, and Ludwig, p. 38; and CIA, "South China Sea" Map.

296. Hong, p. 18; and Valencia, Van Dyke, and Ludwig, p. 34.

297. CIA, "South China Sea" Map; Hong, p. 60; and Valencia, Van Dyke, and Ludwig, p. 53.

298. Hong, p. 132-133; CIA, "South China Sea" Map; Valencia, Van Dyke, and Ludwig, p. 98; Shicun Wu, p. 365; and Amer, "Claims and Conflict Situation," p. 36. At least with China's historic claim, some authors do not believe there is a physical overlap between claims or that it is not yet determined if there is a conflict. Wiencek and Baker, "Security Risks of a South China Sea Conflict"; Joyner; Dolven, Kan, and Manyin, pp. 10, 26; and Greenfield, p. 30.

299. Hong, p. 65.

300. Hong, p. 70; Malaysia and the Socialist Republic of Vietnam, "Executive Summary," *Submission to the Commission on the Limits of the Continental Shelf,* Hanoi, North Vietnam: Ministry of Foreign Affairs, April 2009, p. 5, available from *www.un.org/depts/los/clcs_new/submissions_files/vnm37_09/vnm2009n_executivesummary.pdf.*

301. Valencia, Van Dyke, and Ludwig, p. 50.

302. *Exclusive Economic Zone and Continental Shelf Act*, Beijing, China: Standing Committee of the Ninth National People's Congress, June 26, 1998, Article 12, available from *www.un.org/Depts/los/LEGISLATIONANDTREATIES/PDFFILES/chn_1998_eez_act.pdf*; and *Law on the Exclusive Economic Zone and the Continental Shelf of the Republic of China*, Taipei, Taiwan: Government of the Republic of China, January 21, 1998, Article 4, available from *en.wikisource.org/wiki/Law_on_the_Exclusive_Economic_Zone_and_the_Continental_Shelf_of_the_Republic_of_China*.

303. Dolven, Kan, and Manyin, p. 32; Fravel, p. 35; Dutton, p. 210; Xue, p. 193; and O'Rourke, *China Naval Modernization*, pp. i, 8.

304. This clause covers the special case of passage through straits, but is also found in Article 19 on innocent passage through territorial waters, and Article 301 on peaceful uses of the seas. UN, *UNCLOS*, pp. 31, 37, and 138; and Dutton, p. 211.

305. Lai, *The United States and China in Power Transition*, p. 121; and Fravel, p. 35.

306. UN, *UNCLOS*, p. 44; Dutton, p. 212; and Yongming Jin, "How to Resolve the South China Sea Issue," *China Daily*, July 7, 2011, available from *www.chinadaily.com.cn/cndy/2011-07/07/content_12850748.htm*.

307. UN, *UNCLOS*, p. 44; and Dutton, p. 212.

308. The Congressional Research Service reported 27 countries. Lai states 14 countries ban foreign militaries from their EEZs, O'Rourke cites a study of 18, and Dolven, Kan, and Manyin cite 26 countries but state that Vietnam has relaxed its previous requirement from approval to notification. See O'Rourke, *Maritime Territorial and Exclusive Economic Zone (EEZ) Disputes Involving China*, p. 4; Lai, *The United States and China in Power Transition*, p. 121; Dolven, Kan, and Manyin, p. 32; and ICG, "The South China Sea (II)," p. 11. Taiwan's Foreign Ministry, in a June 2011 press release, seemed to emphasize its support for the U.S. position on the principle of freedom of navigation. See Sutter and Huang, p. 70.

309. Hong, p. 89; Dutton, p. 210; and Xue, pp. 181, 184.

310. Dutton, p. 215.

311. Greenfield, p. 36; and Valencia, Van Dyke, and Ludwig, p. 24.

312. Timo Koivurova, "Power Politics or Orderly Development?" Silverburg, ed., *International Law*, p. 365; and UN, *1958 Geneva Conventions on the Law of the Sea*, p. 312.

313. Adjudicated in the *North Sea Continental Shelf* cases. This decision sparked the need for the third UN Conference on the Law of Sea starting in 1973, and producing the current version of the Law of the Sea Treaty in 1982. Tonnesson, "History of the Dispute," p. 14; and Van Dyke and Bennett, p. 81.

314. Koivurova, pp. 364-365; and Tonnesson, "History of the Dispute," p. 14. Although UNCLOS refers to this region as the continental shelf, in geographic terms it is the continental margin which consists of the relatively flat and shallow continental shelf and the continental slope that drops to the deeper ocean floor. This distinction is relevant because the two defining factors for the extent of the legal continental shelf (the term this monograph will use in accord with UNCLOS) are either: shall not exceed 350 nautical miles from the baselines from which the breadth of the territorial sea is measured; or shall not exceed 100 nautical miles from the 2,500 meter isobath, which is a line connecting the depth of 2,500 metres. UN, *UNCLOS*, p. 53.

315. Valencia, Van Dyke, and Ludwig, p. 37.

316. UN, *UNCLOS*, pp. 54-55.

317. Tonnesson, "History of the Dispute," p. 14.

318. Koivurova, p. 365.

319. Hong, p. 60; and Fravel, p. 36.

320. Fravel, pp. 36-37.

321. Hong, pp. 60-61.

322. Vidas, p. 340; and Valencia, Van Dyke, and Ludwig, p. 50.

323. Hong, p. 55; Valencia, Van Dyke, and Ludwig, pp. 8, 36; USEIA, "South China Sea"; Joyner; and Amer, "Claims and Conflict Situations," p. 27.

324. Hong, pp. 13, 19; and Valencia, Van Dyke, and Ludwig, p. 36.

325. Reefs are natural formations in the ocean that come up to or just below the water's surface, and as such are usually considered to be hazards to navigation. Their characteristic of having no permanent feature above sea level means that under customary law they may not be claimed as sovereign territory, although a state could have jurisdiction rights assigned by UNCLOS over submerged objects in the continental shelf area. Malaysia may claim up to five of these features, the most important Swallow Reef, while Amboyna Cay is claimed by another state, Vietnam.

326. Amer, "Claims and Conflict Situations," pp. 28-29; Shicun Wu, p. 368; and Joyner.

327. Shicun Wu, p. 368; USEIA, "South China Sea"; Valencia, Van Dyke, and Ludwig, p. 38; and Joyner.

328. Hong, p. 18; Van Dyke and Bennett, pp. 74-75; Valencia, Van Dyke and Ludwig, p. 33; and Joyner.

329. Hong, p. 19; Valencia, Van Dyke and Ludwig, pp. 36-37; and Joyner.

330. Greenfield, p. 35; Hong, pp. 18-20; CIA, South China Sea Map; and Valencia, Van Dyke and Ludwig, pp. 35, 48.

331. Malaysia and Socialist Republic of Vietnam, "Executive Summary," *Joint Submission to the Commission on the Limits of the Continental Shelf Pursuant to Article 76, Paragraph 8 of the United Nations Convention on the Law of the Sea 1982 in Respect of the*

Southern Part of the South China Sea, Kuala Lumpur, Malaysia, and Hanoi, North Vietnam: Malaysia's National Security Council and Vietnam's Ministry of Foreign Affairs, May 2009, p. 5, available from *www.un.org/depts/los/clcs_new/submissions_files/mysvnm33_09/mys_vnm2009excutivesummary.pdf*.

332. CIA, "South China Sea" Map. A 2,500 meter deep isobaths line traces the outline of the Spratly Islands along much of its northwest, north, and southeast. The region southwest of the Spratlys, the gap between Borneo and peninsular Malaysia, is not so deep. However, there is also no northwest-to-southeast coast line within 350-nm of the Spratlys within that gap that could claim any of this region through an extended continental shelf.

333. Socialist Republic of Vietnam, "Executive Summary," p. 5; Malaysia and Socialist Republic of Vietnam, "Executive Summary," p. 5; Valencia, Van Dyke, and Ludwig, p. 48; and Amer, "Claims and Conflict Situations," p. 32.

334. USEIA, "South China Sea"; and Amer, "Claims and Conflict Situations," p. 31.

335. Greenfield, p. 40.

336. Valencia, Van Dyke, and Ludwig, p. 48; and Dolven, Kan, and Manyin, p. 11.

337. Valencia, Van Dyke and Ludwig, p. 27; Greenfield, pp. 38-39; and CIA, "South China Sea" Map.

338. Greenfield, pp. 38-39; Van Dyke and Bennett, p. 73; Fravel, p. 37; and CIA, "South China Sea" Map.

339. Valencia, Van Dyke and Ludwig, p. 134.

340. CIA, "The South China Sea" Map; Joyner.

341. UN, *UNCLOS*, p. 67, and Valencia, Van Dyke, and Ludwig, p. 58.

342. Paal, "Territorial Disputes in Asian Waters."

343. Jin; and ICG, "The South China Sea (II)," p. 29.

344. Shicun Wu, p. 365; Joyner; and Greenfield, p. 34.

345. Hong, p. 66.

346. Joyner.

347. Fravel, pp. 35-36.

348. Valencia, Van Dyke, and Ludwig, p. 44.

349. Dolven, Kan, and Manyin, p. 31.

350. Joyner.

351. ICG, "The South China Sea (II)," p. 29.

352. O'Rourke, *China Naval Modernization,* p. 44; and Steven Metz, "Strategic Horizons: U.S. Must Change its Thinking on Conflict in Asia," *World Politics Review,* December 12, 2012, available from *www.worldpoliticsreview.com/articles/12561/strategic-horizons-u-s-must-change-its-thinking-on-conflict-in-asia.*

353. Dolven, Kan, and Manyin, pp. i-ii.

354. Hillary Rodham Clinton, "Remarks at Press Availability," Hanoi, Vietnam: National Convention Center, July 23, 2010, available from *www.state.gov/secretary/rm/2010/07/145095.htm*; and Lai, *The United States and China in Power Transition,* p. 140.

355. Xinbo Wu, *China and the United States: Core Interests, Common Interests, and Partnership,* Washington, DC: United States Institute of Peace, June 2011, pp. 1-2; and Clinton.

356. Kivimaki, Odgaard, and Tonnesson, p. 151.

357. Fravel, p. 47; and Constance Johnson, "China/Vietnam: South China Sea Agreement," Washington, DC: The Law Library of Congress, October 11, 2011, available from *www.loc.gov/lawweb/servlet/lloc_news?disp3_l205402849_text.*

358. Paal, "Dangerous Shoals."

359. Hong, p. 84; and Department of State, "Maritime Security and Navigation," Washington, DC: Bureau of Oceans and International Environment, available from *www.state.gov/e/oes/ocns/opa/maritimesecurity/*.

360. Lai, *The United States and China in Power Transition*, p. 120; Fravel, p. 35; USEIA, "South China Sea"; and Hong, p. 30.

361. Fravel, p. 35; Shicun Wu, pp. 369-371; Xue, p. 184; O'Rourke, *Maritime Territorial and Exclusive Economic Zone (EEZ) Disputes Involving China*, p. 5; and Dolven, Kan, and Manyin, p. 23.

362. Kivimaki, Odgaard, and Tonnesson, p. 140; and Wiencek and Baker, "Security Risks of a South China Sea Conflict."

363. Moller, p. 75; Valencia, Van Dyke, and Ludwig, p. 131; and Hong, p. 84.

364. ICG, "The South China Sea (II)," p. 24.

365. Dolven, Kan, and Manyin, p. 32. Vietnam established a new national *Law on the Sea* in July 2012 which also clarified its maritime jurisdictions, its desires to peacefully settle the disputes, and reiterated its claims over the Paracel and Spratly Islands, increasing tensions again with China. Loi Huynh, "Vietnam: New National Law Intensifies International Dispute," Washington, DC: The Law Library of Congress, July 19, 2012, available from *www.loc.gov/lawweb/servlet/lloc_news?disp3_l205403248_text*.

366. Dutton, p. 213; and Bernard Moreland, "US-China Civil Maritime Operational Engagement," Erickson, Goldstein, and Nan Li, eds., p. 168.

367. Lai, *The United States and China in Power Transition*, p. 119.

368. Moreland, pp. 168-169; and Dutton, p. 225.

369. Zbigniew Bzezinski, "Balancing the East, Upgrading the West: U.S. Grand Strategy in an Age of Upheaval," *Foreign Affairs*, Vol. 91, No. 1, January-February 2012, p. 101; and O'Rourke, *Maritime Territorial and EEZ Disputes*, pp. 49-50.

370. Eric A. McVadon, "Humanitarian Operations: A Window to US-China Maritime Cooperation," Erickson, Goldstein, and Nan Li, eds., p. 266.

371. This agreement was renewed as the *United States/Russian Federation Incidents at Sea and Dangerous Military Activities Agreement* in 1998 and is still enforced. Chief of Naval Operations, "United States/Russian Federation Incidents at Sea and Dangerous Military Activities Agreement," OPNAVINST 5711.96C, Washington, DC: Headquarters, U.S. Navy N3/N5, November 10, 2008, available from *www.fas.org/irp/doddir/navy/opnavinst/5711_96c.pdf*.

372. Lai, *The United States and China in Power Transition*, p. 122; and Bateman, p. 228.

373. Griffiths, p. 43; Hong, p. 89.

374. Shicun Wu, p. 371; and Jin.

375. McVadon, p. 266.

376. Shicun Wu, p. 372; and Huayou Zhu, "Enhancing Sino-US Maritime Security Cooperation in Southeast Asia," Erickson, Goldstein, and Nan Li, eds., p. 283.

377. Shicun Wu, p. 371; and Xue, p. 184.

378. Dolven, Kan, and Manyin, p. ii.

379. Dutton, p. 223; and Goldstein, p. 127.

380. Dutton, p. 223; McVadon, pp. 280-281; Fravel, p. 46; and Moreland, p. 154.

381. Collins, p. 31.

382. Indeed, the U.S. Army has already jump-started the process of gaining regional expertise in a variety of other ways. Training and Doctrine Command (TRADOC) has formed the TRADOC Cultural Center (TCC), expanded operations at the Defense Language Institute Foreign Language Center (DLIFLC)

and developed the University of Foreign Military and Cultural Studies (UFMCS). See Scott G. Wuestner, *Building Partner Capacity/Security Force Assistance: A New Structural Paradigm,* Carlisle Barracks, PA: Strategic Studies Institute, U.S. Army War College, 2009, pp.12-13, available from *www.strategicstudiesinstitute.army. mil/pubs/display.cfm?pubID=880.* In September 2012, the Army also reopened the Military Accessions Vital to the National Interest (MAVINI) fast track to citizenship program meant to recruit native speakers in 47 languages, six of which are spoken in the South China Sea region: Cebuano, Mandarin, Indonesian, Malay, Moro, Tausug, Maranao, Maguindanao, and Tagolog. See Department of the Army (MAVINI). Proper recruitment, management, and retention of so many selected skills will be a challenge to the Institutional Army, as it may already have realized through the challenge of managing its Special Forces soldiers, and will require a sustained investment in money and resources. See Steve Griffin, "Regionally-Aligned Brigades: There's More to This Plan Than Meets the Eye," *Small Wars Journal,* September 19, 2012, available from *smallwarsjournal.com/jrnl/art/regionally-aligned-brigades-theres-more-to-this-plan-than-meets-the-eye.* Also see Wuestner; Department of the Army, "MAVINI Information Sheet," Washington, DC: U.S. Department of the Army, Office of the Assistant Secretary for Manpower and Reserve Affairs, undated, available from *www.goarmy.com/content/dam/goarmy/downloaded_assets/ mavni/mavni-language.pdf;* Griffin; David Vergun, "Army Partnering for Peace," U.S. Army New Service, October 25, 2012, available from *www.army.mil/article/90010/Army_partnering_for_peace__ security/;* and United States Army, "Regional Alignment in Joint and Combined Exercises," *Stand To,* August 28, 2013, available from *www.army.mil/standto/archive_2013-08-28/?s_cid=standto.*

383. John Vandiver, "AFRICOM First to Test New Regional Brigade Concept," *Stars and Stripes,* May 17, 2012, available from *www.stripes.com/news/africom-first-to-test-new-regional-brigade-concept-1.177476;* and Vergun.

384. Otto Kreisher, "DOD Too Cautious: 'We Have to be Willing to Fail,' Says Flournoy," *AOL Defense.Com,* December 12, 2012, available from *defense.aol.com/2012/12/12/dod-too-cautious-we-have-to-be-willing-to-fail-says-flournoy.*

385. Raymond T. Odierno, *2012 Army Strategic Planning Guidance,* Washington, DC: U.S. Department of the Army, April 19, 2012, p. 6, available from *usarmy.vo.llnwd.net/e2/c/downloads/243816.pdf.*

386. Dunnigan, James, "If It Works for Special Forces . . ." *Strategy Page,* October 8, 2012, available from *www.strategypage.com/dls/articles/If-It-Works-For-Special-Forces...-10-8-2012.asp.*

387. "Active Component Army Civil Affairs Units," Civil Affairs Association, available from *www.civilaffairsassoc.org/civilaffairsassociation/our-nations-civil-affairs-units/active-component-army-civil-affairs-units/;* and "364th Civil Affairs Brigade (Airborne)," GlobalSecurity, available from *www.globalsecurity.org/military/agency/army/364ca-bde.htm.*

388. Michelle Tan, "1st Regionally Aligned BCT to Deploy to Africa," *Military Times,* February 20, 2013, available from *www.militarytimes.com/article/20130220/NEWS/302200333/1st-regionally-aligned-BCT-deploy-Africa;* and Vergun.

389. *State Partnership Program: Improved Oversight, Guidance, and Training Needed for National Guard's Efforts with Foreign Partners,* Washington, DC: U.S. Government Accountability Office, (USGAO) May 2012, p. 9, available from *www.gao.gov/assets/600/590840.pdf.*

390. Vergun; and USGAO, p. 36.

391. "Oregon National Guard, Vietnam Sign Partnership Pact," Armed Forces Press Service (AFPS), November 30, 2012, available from *www.defense.gov/News/NewsArticle.aspx?ID=118666.*

392. USGAO, pp. 2, 7-9; and AFPS, "Oregon National Guard."

393. Paul McLeary, "U.S. Unit's Africa Deployment Will Test New Regional Concept," *Defense News Online,* September 26, 2012, available from *www.defensenews.com/article/20120926/DEFREG04/309260003/U-S-Unit-8217-s-Africa-Deployment-Will-Test-New-Regional-Concept.*

394. Tan.

395. McLeary.

396. David J. Berteau and Michael J. Green *et al.*, *U.S. Force Posture Strategy in the Asia Pacific Region: An Independent Assessment*, Washington, DC: Center for Strategic and International Studies, 2012, pp. 91-92, available from *csis.org/files/publication/120814_FINAL_PACOM_optimized.pdf*.

397. ICG, "The South China Seas (II)" p. 10.

398. Berteau and Green, p. 91.

399. Griffin; and Dan Cox, "An Enhanced Plan for Regionally Aligning Brigades Using Human Terrain Systems," *Small Wars Journal*, June 14, 2012, available from *smallwarsjournal.com/jrnl/art/an-enhanced-plan-for-regionally-aligning-brigades-using-human-terrain-systems*.

400. Giffin; and Wuestner, pp. 14-16, 36-37.

401. Griffin.

402. Mcleary. These phases refer to DoD's six phases of the Continuum of Military Operations. Phase 0 is Shape the Environment, Phase 1 is Deter the Enemy, and Phase 2 is Seize the Initiative.

403. Berteau and Green, p. 90.

404. Vandiver.

405. Roger Rufe, "Statement of Roger Rufe, President of the Ocean Conservancy (Private)," Testimony before the Senate Committee on Foreign Relations, Washington, DC, October 21, 2003, pp. 2-3, available from *www.foreign.senate.gov/imo/media/doc/Rufe-Testimony031021.pdf*.

406. Dolven, Kan, and Manyin, p. 32.

407. *Ibid.*, pp. ii, 5; Clinton; and Shearer, p. 200.

408. Dolven, Kan, and Manyin, p. 32; Fravel, p. 35; and O'Rourke, *Maritime Territorial and EEZ Disputes*, p. 4.

409. Shearer, p. 219. One major historic maritime claim's case settled by the International Court of Justice was the Gulf of Fonseca case in 1992. This was different, however, because the surrounding geography of the Gulf of Fonseca was a minor bay between Honduras, Nicaragua, and El Salvador, and the claims stemmed from an established unified claim from the Federal Republic of Central America. After the demise of the Federal Republic in 1839, this claim was not defined among its subsequent members. This would not be a good precedent for the South China Sea, which is more open and never had a recognized unified claim. Valencia, Van Dyke, and Ludwig, p. 17.

410. Hong, pp. 70-71.

411. Valencia, Van Dyke, and Ludwig, p. 26.

412. *Ibid.*, p. 25; Shearer, p. 208; and Clinton.

413. Clinton.

414. ICG, "The South China Sea (II)," pp. 29-30; Swaine, p. 10; and USEIA, "South China Sea."

415. Valencia, Van Dyke, and Ludwig, p. 78.

416. Hong, p. 67.

417. Hong, p. 63. This split of rights would be similar to the Torres Strait Treaty negotiated between Papua New Guinea and Australia in 1978. Here the inhabitants of Australian islands in the EEZ of Papua New Guinea were given rights to fish in the area but other rights were kept for the coastal EEZ state. Van Dyke and Bennett, p. 83.

418. Paal, "Dangerous Shoals."

419. *Ibid.*; and Valencia, Van Dyke, and Ludwig, p. 78.

420. Hong, p. 30; and ICG, "The South China Sea (II)," p. 4.

421. Valencia, Van Dyke, and Ludwig, p. 1.

422. Amer, "Ongoing Efforts in Conflict Management," p. 120; and ICG, "The South China Sea (II)," p. 30.

423. Lai, *The United States and China in Power Transition*, p. 140.

424. USPACOM, p. 2.

425. USEIA, "South China Sea"; and Fravel, p. 35. Not challenging commercial transit through historic waters does present a dilemma for Chinese and Vietnamese claims. Allowing uncontrolled passage undercuts their historic claims, since historic waters should be governed as closely as internal sovereign waterways. However, to regulate free passage in one of the world's busiest waterways would unleash an international outcry and action that could eliminate any support for their current assertions and remove historic waters as a bargaining position. This is an example of why international approbation is a necessary part of the International Court of Justice's criteria for granting historic waters status. Valencia, Van Dyke, and Ludwig, p. 28.

426. UN, *UNCLOS*, p. 25.

427. For instance, in Article 116, "Right to Fish on the High Seas," and Articles 186 to 191 under the "Settlement of Disputes and Advisory Options" section pertaining to the Seabed Disputes Chamber of the International Tribunal of the Law of the Sea. UN, *UNCLOS*, pp. 65, 95-97.

428. Valencia, Van Dyke, and Ludwig, p. 146. In the same vein, Article 82 requires coastal states to also make a payment of 1 to 7 percent on the value or volume of production from the continental shelf area between 200 and 350-nm offshore which is the extended continental shelf that reaches into otherwise international waters. UN, *UNCLOS*, pp. 55-56.

429. *Ibid.*, p. 67.

430. Valencia, Van Dyke, and Ludwig, p. 146; Chinkin, p. 249; and Xue, p. 176.

431. Studeman.

432. Valencia, Van Dyke, and Ludwig, pp. 55-56.

433. *Ibid.*, pp. 31, 56, 264; CIA, "South China Sea" Map.

434. Valencia, Van Dyke, and Ludwig, p. 265.

435. Joyner.

436. Other objectionable economic provisions concerning mandatory transfer of technology and production limitations were not enforced. Shearer, p. 200; and Rufe.

437. Hong, p. 139; and Dolven, Kan, and Manyin, p. 33.

438. Three reasons account for the lack of commercial success in mining polymetallic seabed nodules which were the target of the ISA regime. First is the high cost and technical difficulty of mounting such operations under the extreme conditions of open ocean and abysmal depths. Second is the continuing relative low cost of competing land based sources. Third is the additional cost levied by the ISA as a "tax" to pay for its administration and to distribute to states around the world. "Manganese Nodule," *Wikipedia*, available from *en.wikipedia.org/wiki/Manganese_nodule*.

439. Hong, p. 2.

440. Valencia, Van Dyke, and Ludwig, pp. 3, 215.

441. Kivimaki, Odgaard, and Tonnesson, p. 152; Valencia, Van Dyke, and Ludwig, pp. 183-184; and CIA, South China Sea Map.

442. Also known as the Spitzbergen Islands Treaty for the former name of this Arctic Ocean archipelago, Norway was awarded sovereignty based on its association with and proximity to the islands. However, the islands had long been used by many other states as a common area, and the treaty allows the citizens of any ratifying state to take up residence and economic endeavors on the islands under Norwegian law and the stipulations of the treaty. There are 25 states in the treaty, including the United States, Russia, China, India, Japan, New Zealand, Saudi Arabia, and Afghanistan. See Valencia, Van Dyke, and Ludwig, pp. 182-183.

443. *Ibid.*, pp. 182-183.

444. *Ibid.*, pp. 206, 218-219.

445. Clinton.

446. Valencia, Van Dyke, and Ludwig, pp. 171-172.

447. *Ibid.*, p. 179; and Greenfield, p. 39-40.

448. Ness, p. 46.

449. Valencia, Van Dyke, and Ludwig, pp. 45, 56, 205.

450. Normally this is interpreted to mean shelving the maritime jurisdiction disputes not those over island sovereignty. Fravel, p. 45; and Hong, p. 181.

451. Hong, p. 30.

452. *Ibid.*, p. 185.

453. ICG, "The South China Sea (II)," p. 6.

454. Dolven, Kan, and Manyin, p. 30; Clinton; and Hong, p. 14.

455. Dolven, Kan, and Manyin, p. 11; Hong, p. 14; and Jin.

456. Valencia, Van Dyke, and Ludwig, p. 97; Dolven, Kan, and Manyin, p. 26; ICG, "The South China Sea (II)," p. 7; and Trillanes, p. 7.

457. Studeman.

458. ICG, "The South China Sea (II)," p. 34.

459. Valencia, Van Dyke, and Ludwig, p. 101.

460. Clinton.

461. Kreisher.

462. Paal, "Territorial Disputes in Asian Waters"; and Dolven, Kan, and Manyin, pp. i-ii.

463. Hong, p. 197.

464. Brzezinski, p. 97.

465. Jianzhong Zhuang, "China's Maritime Development and US-China Cooperation," Erickson, Goldstein, and Nan Li, eds., p. 8.

466. "China, U.S. Pledge to Build Constructive Strategic Partnership," Washington, DC: Embassy of the People's Republic of China, April 1999, available from *www.china-embassy.org/eng/zmgx/zysj/zrjfm/t36212.htm*; and Erikson and Goldstein, p. xi.

467. Fravel, p. 47; and Paal, "Territorial Disputes in Asian Waters."

468. *Maritime Security Policy*, National Security Presidential Directive 41, Washington, DC: The White House, December 21, 2004, available from *https:// www.fas.org/irp/offdocs/nspd/nspd41.pdf*; and Dutton, p. 197.

469. USPACOM, pp. 3-5.

470. Clinton.

471. Erickson, p. 431.

472. Valencia, Van Dyke, and Ludwig, p. 5; and Hong, p. 198.

473. Moller, p. 75; Amer, "Ongoing Efforts in Conflict Management," p. 123; and Kivimaki, Odgaard, and Tonnesson, p. 146.

474. Valencia, Van Dyke, and Ludwig, p. 111.

475. Kivimaki, Odgaard, and Tonnesson, p. 143; Wiencek and Baker, "Security Risks of a South China Sea Conflict"; Erickson, p. 431; Xinbo Wu, *US Security Policy in Asia: Implications for China-US Relations*, Washington, DC: The Brookings Institution, September

2000, available from *www.brookings.edu/research/papers/2000/09/northeastasia-xinbo*; and Dutton, p. 208.

476. Wiencek and Baker, "Security Risks of a South China Sea Conflict"; and Paal, "Dangerous Shoals."

477. Wu, *US Security Policy in Asia: Implications for China-US Relations.*

478. Kivimaki, Odgaard, and Tonnesson, pp. 139-140; Shicun Wu, pp. 368-369; and Wu, *US Security Policy in Asia: Implications for China-US Relations.* Following the Mischief Reef incident:

> on 16 June 1995 . . . Joseph Nye, then US Assistant Secretary of Defense for International Security, said, 'if military action occurred in the Spratleys and this interfered with the freedom of the seas, then we would be prepared to escort and make sure that navigation continues.' This was the first time that a US high-level official expressed the possibility of US military intervention on the SCS issue on the basis of its interference with navigation.

Shicun Wu, p. 369.

479. Lai, *The United States and China in Power Transition,* pp. 137, 143.

480. Lai, *The United States and China in Power Transition,* p. 137; Hong, p. 196; and Kivimaki, Odgaard, and Tonnesson, pp. 142-143, 147.

481. Such conflict includes PRC involvement in the Korean War:

> shelling of the Taiwanese-occupied offshore islands of Quemoy in 1958, the PRC's brief war with India in 1962, the border skirmishes with the Soviet Union in 1969, and the PRC invasion of Vietnam in 1979.

Kivimaki, Odgaard, and Tonnesson, p. 144.

482. Controversy from remarks made by mid-level Chinese officials in 2010 have left uncertain if one of the PRC's declared core interests of sovereignty over China's territory, which it considers non-negotiable, also includes the Spratly Islands. If, indeed, that was not the intent of the Chinese government, some believe that China's interests are nonetheless moving in that direction. Swaine, p. 2; Fravel, p. 42; and Jisi Wang, "China's Search for a Grand Strategy: A Rising Great Power Finds Its Way," *Foreign Affairs*, Vol. 90, No. 2, March-April 2011, pp. 70-71.

483. Kivimaki, Odgaard, and Tonnesson, pp. 134-135; and Moller, p. 76.

484. Dolven, Kan, and Manyin, p. 28; Valencia, Van Dyke, and Ludwig, p. 80; Hong, p. 140; Kivimaki, Odgaard, and Tonnesson, p. 140; and "U.S. Reaffirms Defense Treaty with Philippines," *The Peninsula*, Qatar, June 1, 2013, available from *thepeninsulaqatar. com/latest-news/239548-us-reaffirms-defence-treaty-with-philippines. html*.

485. Valencia, p. 440.

486. "Southeast Asia Treaty Organization," in *West's Encyclopedia of American Law*, Farmington Hills, MI: The Gale Group, 2008, available from *legal-dictionary.thefreedictionary.com/Southeast +Asia+Collective+Defense+Treaty*.

487. ICG, "The South China Sea (II)," p. 32; Kivimaki, Odgaard, and Tonnesson, p. 139; and USPACOM, pp. 2-3.

488. Brzezinski, pp. 99-100.

489. ICG, "The South China Sea (II)," p. 25; and Paal, "Dangerous Shoals."

490. These include a myriad of activities including frequent presence of U.S. naval ships in the region; the expansion of military bases on the U.S. island territory of Guam; access rights in Thailand (U-Tapao), Malaysia, (Lumut), Indonesia (Surabaya), and Australia (Darwin); naval exercises with Vietnam through a budding military relationship; Singapore expanding Changi naval base to accommodate the Seventh Fleet with the permanent

basing of a U.S. logistics unit there; a tripling of port calls to Malaysia over 10 years; and an agreement for U.S. Forces to again access the Philippine's Clark and Subic Bay bases, along with much needed enhanced bilateral security cooperation, such as a land based radar to track ships and Hamilton class cutters. Kivimaki, Odgaard, and Tonnesson, pp. 141-142; Shicun Wu, p. 370; Wu, *US Security Policy in Asia: Implications for China-US Relations*; Moller, p. 76; Pan; Hong, pp. 28, 30, 196-198; ICG; "The South China Sea (II)," pp. 11, 26; Dolven, Kan, and Manyin, p. 29; and Jamie Laude, "US Troops Can Use Clark, Subic Bases," *The Philippine Star*, June 6, 2012, available from *www.ajdigitaledition.com/pdfs/PDF/2012_LA/2012_06_09/2012_LA_06_09_A%2014.pdf*.

491. Pan.

492. Paal, "Dangerous Shoals."

493. Shicun Wu, p. 370; and Lai, *The United States and China in Power Transition*, p. 140.

494. Kivimaki, Odgaard, and Tonnesson, p. 147; and Valencia, Van Dyke, and Ludwig, p. 92.

495. Kivimaki, Odgaard, and Tonnesson, p. 141.

496. *Ibid.*, pp. 135, 147.

497. ICG, "The South China Sea (II)," p. 25.

498. Dolven, Kan, and Manyin, p. 23; Fravel, p. 47.

499. Valencia, Van Dyke, and Ludwig, p. 131.

500. Hong, p. 30.

501. ICG, "South China Sea (II)," p. 27.

502. Valencia, Van Dyke, and Ludwig, p. 99.

503. Brzezinski, p. 97.